TOTAL QUALITY MANAGEMENT FOR THE FOOD INDUSTRIES

by
Wilbur A. Gould, Ph.D.
Food Industries Consultant
Emeritus Professor of Food Processing & Technology,
Department of Horticulture,
Ohio State University,
Ohio Agricultural Research & Development Center,
Former Director, Food Industries Center,
The Ohio State University and
Executive Director Mid-America Food Processors Association,
Worthington, Ohio

CTI Publications, Inc.
2 Oakway Road, Timonium, Maryland 21093-4247 USA
Voice 410-308-2080   FAX 410-308-2079

CTI Publications, Inc.
2 Oakway Road, Timonium, Maryland 21093-4247 USA
Voice 410-308-2080   FAX 410-308-2079

© **COPYRIGHT 1992 by CTI Publications, Inc.**
Baltimore, Maryland
Printed in The United States Of America

ISBN Numbers are as follows:
0-930027-19-1

Library of Congress Cataloging – in – Publication Data

Gould Wilbur A., 1920–
   Total quality management for the food industries/by Wilbur A. Gould.
      p.   cm.
   Includes bibliographical references and index.
   ISBN 0-930027-19-1 (hard)
   1. Food industry and trade – Quality control. 2. Total quality management. I.
Title
TP372.5.G69 1992   92-11409
664'.068'5--dc20   CIP

While the recommendations in this publication are based on scientific studies and wide industry experience, references to basic principles, operating procedures and methods, or types of instruments and equipment are not be construed as a guarantee that they are sufficient to prevent damage, spoilage, loss, accidents or injuries, resulting from use of this information. Furthermore, the study and use of this publication by any person or company is not to be considered as assurance that a person or company is proficient in the operations and procedures discussed in this publication. The use of the statements, recommendations, or suggestions contained, herein, is not to be considered as creating any responsibility for damage, spoilage, loss, accident or injury, resulting from such use.

CTI Publications, Inc.
2 Oakway Road, Timonium, Maryland 21093-4247 USA
Voice 410-308-2080   FAX 410-308-2079

Other Title's From CTI Publications

FOOD PRODUCTION/MANAGEMENT editorially serves those in the Canning, Glasspacking, Freezing and Aseptic Packaged Food Industries.

Editorial topics cover the range of Basic Management Policies, from the growing of the Raw Products through Processing, Production and Distribution for the following products: fruits; vegetables; dried and dehydrated fruit (including vegetables and soup mixes); juices, preserves; pickles and pickled products; sauces and salad dressings; catsup and tomato products; soups; cured fish and seafood, baby foods; seasonings and other specialty items. (Monthly Magazine). ISSN: 0191-6181

A COMPLETE COURSE IN CANNING, 12th edition, are technical reference and textbooks for Students of Food Technology; Food Plant Managers; Products Research and Development Specialists; Food Equipment Manufacturers and Salesmen; Brokers; and Food Industry Suppliers. The three books total 1,300 pages. ISBN: 0-930027-00-0.

TOTAL QUALITY ASSURANCE FOR THE FOOD INDUSTRIES is 400 pages of A to Z technology and practical application of the latest methods and detailed procedure in developing total quality assurance in all food plants, including sanitary standards, as well as bacteriological procedures. This is the complete instruction book, easily followed, yet technically complete for the advanced Food Technologist. ISBN: 0-930027-14-0.

CURRENT GOOD MANUFACTURING PRACTICES/FOOD PLANT SANI-TATION covers all Current Food Manufacturing practices as prescribed by the United States Department of Agriculture, Food and Drug Administration, as it applies to food processing and manufacturing. A total of 21 chapters, covering all phases of sanitation. ISBN: 0-930027-15-9.

GLOSSARY FOR THE FOOD INDUSTRIES is a definitive list of food abbreviations, terms, terminologies and acronyms. Also included are 20 handy reference tables and charts for the food industry. ISBN: 0-930027-16-7.

RESEARCH & DEVELOPMENT GUIDELINES FOR THE FOOD INDUSTRIES is a compilation of all Research and Development principles and objectives. Easily understood by the student or the professional this text is a practical "How To Do It and Why To Do It" reference. ISBN: 0-930027-17-5.

TOMATO PRODUCTION, PROCESSING & TECHNOLOGY, 3rd edition, is a book needed by all tomato and tomato products packers, growers, or anyone involved or interested in packing, processing, and production of tomatoes and tomato products. ISBN: 0-930027-18-3.

For a brochure or further information on the above publications please contact:

CTI Publications, Inc.
2 Oakway Road, Timonium, Maryland 21093-4247 USA

This copy of
**Total Quality Management
For The Food Industries**
belongs to:

_____

PREFACE

I have spent much of my life time teaching, researching, and writing of and about quality, quality evaluation, quality control, quality assurance, quality auditing, and the importance of quality to a food firm. All of this has been most important in the development of high quality products from the food industries. However, in many cases the quality effort has been a policing program and not a direct responsibility of the individual operator. Times have changed during these many years and today we must look at total quality from a management standpoint. They are the ones that really control quality. As Dr. Deming has stated on many occasions, 85% of the problems in quality are the responsibility of management. Management must provide the right machinery, materials, methods, and train the manpower for greater quality assurance and improved productivity.

The modern view of quality management is explicitly defined when one looks at the concept and philosophy of Total Quality Management (TQM). TQM is a system of management that gauges a company's dedication to consistent improvement and a sincere effort to serve its customers with what they expect all the time. It is a philosophy of management to achieve greater productivity and a total awareness of quality as an increasingly important element in competitiveness. The firm that understands the requirements for quality excellence is the one that will be on top in this century because they take appropriate steps to fix problems and find solutions to eliminate further problems. Most importantly, the firm that learns to communicate between management and the employees and their customers is the one that will win out. The winner understands and has an obsession for continual improvement and the belief that good is never good enough.

Total Quality Management can be broken down into the three words to reflect on its true and simplest meanings, that is,

TOTAL- means everyone and everything that we do,
QUALITY- means giving the customer what they expect all the time,
MANAGEMENT- means the way we act and operate, our policies and procedures, and our training and instruction to all of our employees.

In these times quality in so important to the customer. Quality to the customer implies the safety of the product, the performance and use of the product, the shelf stability of the product, the compliance of the product with the latest regulations including labeling and education of the user, defect free including all harmful microbes, and, most importantly, complete satisfaction.

Total Quality Management is a system that can help the food industry just like it has helped other firms in manufacturing, service industries, and the many aspects agricultural production firms, etc. It is a system that must not be ignored. It is a system of management that is long overdue and when utilized to its fullest it will return big dividends to the user.

Total Quality Management is the right thing to do. It can and it will be most beneficial to those firms that adopt the fundamentals of TQM and practice the principles.

WILBUR A. GOULD

ABOUT THE AUTHOR

Wilbur A. Gould was reared on a farm in Northern New Hampshire. He received his Batchelor of Science degree from the University of New Hampshire in Horticulture-Plant Breeding. He started his graduate work at Michigan State University prior to service in the U.S. Navy during World War II. After military service, he completed his Master of Science and Ph. D. degrees at The Ohio State University.

Dr. Gould retired from The Ohio State University after 39 years on the faculty as Professor of Food Processing and Technology. He taught 9 courses during his tenure and advised over 900 undergraduate students, 131 Master of Science Students and 76 Doctoral students. His major research interests were in Vegetable Processing and Technology and Snack Food Manufacture and Quality Assurance. He has authored some 83 referred journal research publications, over 200 Food Trade articles, and 9 books.

Dr. Gould is a Member of Phi Kappa Phi, Phi Sigma, Phi Tau Sigma, Sigma Xi, Gamma Sigma Delta (Award of Merit in 1984), Alpha Gamma Rho, Institute of Food Technologists (Fellow in 1982), and American Society of Horticultural Science (Distinguished Graduate Teaching Award in 1985).

The following are some of the recognitions that Dr. Gould has received: The Ohio State University Distinguished Leadership to Students Award in 1963 and a Certificate of Recognition Award in 1986; Ohio Food Processors H.D. Brown Person of Year Award in 1971; Ohio Food Processors Association Tomato Achievement Award in 1985; Ozark Food Processors Association Outstanding Professional Leadership Award in 1978; 49er's Service Award in 1979; Food Processing Machinery and Supplies Association Leadership and Service Award in 1988; Ohio Agricultural Hall of Fame in 1989 and an Honorary Life Membership in Potato Association of America in 1990.

Dr. Gould presently serves as Executive Director of Mid-America Food Processors Association, Food Technology Consultant to the Snack Food Association, Secretary-Treasurer of The Guard Society, and Consultant to the Food Industries.

Dr. Gould's philosophy is to tell it as he sees it, be short and get right to the point.

TOTAL QUALITY MANAGEMENT

by
Wilbur A. Gould

Table Of Contents

CHAPTER 1

Introduction to
Total Quality Management (TQM)

Since the late '40's much has been written and spoken relative to quality control of food processing operations and the evaluation of finished products. In the past ten to fifteen years, emphasis has been placed on quality assurance. The quality Control and quality assurance movement have been a great help to many companies and they have been successful because the products were what they intended them to be.

Today, the quality assurance effort has shifted from the laboratory to the production floor. Today each operator should be trained to operate his or her operation within given specification limits. The operators should understand sampling and know how to collect data continuously and maintain the operation within the limits. If problems arise, the operator should know how to use the tools of total quality management to solve problems in their areas.

More importantly, today's plant employee must be a team player. The team must learn how to be competitive and how to keep score. They have learned the hard way that success comes only from everyone working together. One mistake along the production line carries all the way through to the finished product. The goals and aspiration of the team are always to help each other and to share their strengths and successes together. Strength comes from team work and by working together a firm can become most successful to meet the competition of the present era.

Total Quality Management is the modern term to describe how firms are becoming more successful today. It is a new philosophy that sets the stage for employees working with management, employees having a voice in the operation and employees who feel they are a part of ownership of the firm. Management recognizes the rights of each individual and management knows the meaning of team work.

Results of Total Quality Management (TQM) are significant in productivity gains, unit cost reduction, elimination of much absenteeism, lowering of Worker's Compensation rates, reduction of accidents, elimination of most consumer complaints, and winning consumers by always giving them what they expect.

TQM is more than a buzz word, it's management and employees working together for the good of the firm and the ultimate customer. Slogans, like "Made in America", "People make Candy", "Quality is Job One", or "We are Family" are meaningful expressions of loyalty, cooperation, and fulfillment on the job. John F. Kennedy said "Ask not what your country can do for you, but what you can do for your country". Paraphrasing this statement is what TQM is all about, "ask not what your firm can do for you, but what you can do for your firm". It works and it is leading firms very successfully into the next decade.

In any food firm, people are the most important single asset. People make all the difference in this world and its how they show their enthusiasm about what they do, how they do it, why they do it, and when they do it that makes all the difference. People operate food plants and people make food products acceptable to the customer. People are most important and what we do together makes all the difference between success and failure. People need help, guidance, and in most cases training to move forward. 96% of all people want to do better and its up to management to provide the right environment, guide them through appropriate training, and help them to succeed for the growth of the firm, if the firm wishes to become more successful.

We need to learn to carefully communicate our values and our requirements. People want to know and through the proper use of the spoken and written word, the visual pictures and images, and the physical appearances and signs are all concerned wherein much good can be accomplished. Communication is a two way street. The sender may have a message, but the receiver must understand and comprehend the message or we really haven't communicated.

Lastly, and probably most importantly, every worker in a food plant today must have his or her own "tool box". That tool box must contain tools that will help all employees, that is, the office person, purchasing personnel, production line operators, warehouse personnel, salesmen, marketing manager or even the supervisors and line managers to do their job easier, more reliably, and with unbiased decisions by using observed data. Thus all decisions are based on facts, not hearsay.

Total Quality Management is the only answer to guide a firm, its people, its quality of products, and improve its productivity and provide that service, that product, and that expectation that the customer wants. Every firm that endorses, resources, and practices a Total Quality Management program will find great and meaningful accomplishments today and in the immediate future. Its the right step to achieve excellence and the development of satisfied customers. It will help you to more than meet your competition and build your bottom line.

CHAPTER 2

Philosophy of TQM

Total Quality Management (TQM) is the new kid on the block. It is a process of change and improvement in everything that we do, that is, the products we make, the services we give our customers, the office practices we use, the procurement procedures that we employ and the marketing strategies that we use. TQM is a part of the methods that we employ. Total Quality Management can be defined by understanding each of three words in Total Quality Management separately:

Total-Means everyone must be involved from the office level, through the factory floor and warehouse, marketing and sales, our suppliers, and our customers. Further, total implies everything that we do in the firm, that is, our level of quality, our services, our competitiveness in the market place and our overall image and support we give our employees, our suppliers, our customers, and our public at large.

Quality-The uniform level of the quality of the products that we wish to produce to provide our customers with what they expect with the understanding that we are constantly working to improve quality, but always remaining competitive.

Management-The way we act and work with our employees, our equipment, our processes, our suppliers, our customers, and our public at large.

Separately these words are significant unto themselves, but when we put them together they are the management style we wish to use in the successful operation of our business for continued improvement year after year. TQM is the right approach to beat the competition and lead our firm into the next decade with world class quality and productivity that is equal to or better than the competititon.

The goal of TQM is to seek business excellence and competitive leadership to satisfy our customers expectations. The customer defines and establishes the level of quality they expect and it is up to every firm to realize that what the customer wants is what the customer should get. Every food firm must develop goals, strategic plans, and operational programs to achieve quality leadership.

TQM is the modern way of thinking and creating quality values on which a company must operate. TQM is the modern expression of human excellence. TQM requires the commitment on the part of everyone in the organization. TQM is caring about people, their training, their growth, and their dedication to the success of the firm.

TQM will boost employee moral and a firm's overall productivity. Some state that productivity will increase in excess of some 50% while cost of manufacturing will be lowered by over 50%. Further, some users of TQM show data wherein complaints are cut in half, Worker Compensation reduced by ⅓rd along with comparable numbers for employee turnover and grievance activity. Other users of TQM indicate that total cycle time has been drastically cut and inventories are reduced by many thousands of dollars. TQM does work and it is the modern management technique for todays food processors.

Total Quality Management can be likened to a team sport wherein all the participants must be involved. Quality is truly everybody's business. The interaction of many different talents is required for success. Management must have a conceptual understanding of quality technologies including statistical thinking and utilization of the "tools" of statistical process control. By the same token, technical and production personnel must understand management's role and the management technique that they are now using.

Vince Lombardi, the great coach of the Green Bay Packers football team had a three point formula for being successful in sports, business, and life. In addition to talent and discipline, Lombardi emphasized that, "you have to care for each other. For the entire team to win every time a player makes a move, he has to consider the effect of his move on the rest of the players on the field." Understanding Lombardi's success tells us that we must understand the responsibilities and moves of our fellow worker and, in turn, our fellow workers must understand our responsibilities and our moves as each of our actions will have an effect on each other. Thus, team work is the only answer for controlling quality and becoming more proficient in what we do. If we really think seriously about position in the firm, it should be obvious that team work is a common sense approach and the only approach for the operation of food firms efficiently.

TQM means consistency of action. TQM means dedication to purpose. TQM means significant culture change on the part of everyone in the organization. TQM demands time and resolve. TQM demands determination to make a change for the better.

TQM will boost employee moral. People want to have the internal feeling that they belong, they are a part of the organization, their ideas merit listening too, and that they are contributing to the good of the firm. A firm can boost their moral by helping them feel like they are part of the team, they are part of making the firm more productive, and that they are the ones assuring quality. Belonging is a big part of believing that they are making a contribution. Moral building is a big part of establishing ethics of productivity and quality assurance. It all comes about by having the right habits and proper training.

TQM will help increase a firms market share and help a firm to move forward by becoming more competitive. Finally, TQM has a direct bearing on improving a firms bottom line. TQM will improve the profit margin.

TQM has only 3 barriers for executing a successful quality improvement program: (1) Top Management, (2) Middle Management, and (3) 1st Line Management. Management up and down the line must be committed to change and management must lead the change by setting the example for change. Management must make quality improvement a principal part of their job descriptions, their vocabulary, their attitude, their awareness, and their personal behavior. Management must be visible. Managers must manage by walking around (MBWA). First and foremost managers must be oriented toward understanding human relations. Managers must be cheer-leaders. Managers must be great communicatiors. Managers must be good teachers, Managers must train their people. Managers must be involved in the total operation. Most importantly, managers must have great vision for the firm, its people, its products, and its services.

Successful management in this decade must be flexible and willing to listen to their employees. Management in this decade must create an atmosphere for their firm wherein employees can fully share in the decision process. Management must recognize and reward people for their contributions in the firms success. Management must utilize minds and not just muscle to be successful today.

The first requirement for success with Total Quality Management is for the Chief Executive Officer (CEO) to adopt and set forth the firm's Principles of Operation, their Mission Statement, and their Statement of Purpose. These may be all inclusive or they may be separate documents. They must be written. The must focus on priorities. They must state what the firm stands for with regards to its co-workers and its customers. Most importantly these statements or beliefs must be communicated to all employees and the public at large. These statements or principles of operation become the credo for the firm which all within the firm must learn to understand, respect, and become committed to support and uphold. These statements must be constantly up-dated and communicated to all personnel. Once the values are clearly stated and communicated, people will direct their energies and their enthusiasm toward greater support, productivity, and the manufacture of improved quality products. They are, thus, in direct pursuit of excellence.

The second requirement for Total Quality Management to be successful is for sales and marketing to understand and realize that they are a major part of the total team effort. They must understand that their only purpose is to serve the end use of the products manufactured by the firm, that is, the customer. Sales and marketing personnel are the eyes and ears of the firm to management and the firm and they must recognize their role as partners in the total quality management team effort.

The following is an example of a POLICY STATEMENT for the WAGCO firm that sets forth the Mission, Policy, and Objectives:

Our firm is committed to producing and processing high quality, safe, wholesome, and nutritious food products. We are successful because we care about you, our employees, and our customers whom we serve. We only use safe and approved ingredients and we make our products uniformly. We market our products efficiently and we give our customers a good value for their money. We wish to continue to grow and to that end we believe in supporting research for better raw materials and ingredients, improved processing methods, greater efficiency in manufacturing by using the most modern equipment and procedures, and the constant development of new products for new markets. We believe in maintaining good human relations with our employees, our customers, our suppliers, and the public at large. We will constantly create a positive environment which will nurture personal growth. We believe in giving fair and just treatment to all concerned. We anticipate continued growth and we expect all our employees to contribute to our firm's advancement. Further, we pledge to act responsibly with our fellow workers, our suppliers, our customers, and the community at large.

FIGURE 2.1 — Customer Quality

**YOU ARE IN THE BUSINESS OF
PRODUCING A PRODUCT —
INTENDED FOR SALE TO A
CUSTOMER —
FROM WHICH YOU HOPE TO MAKE A PROFIT.**

KEY WORD IS
CUSTOMER
HE IS THE ONE YOU MUST SATISFY.

THEREFORE,
**THE CUSTOMER ESTABLISHES
THE LEVEL OF QUALITY.**

CHAPTER 3

The Management of TQM

Dr. Deming, considered by many as the Father of the present movement to an effective management system, states that the next component of TQM is establishing "Policies and Procedures" and "Tools" following an understanding of the "right Philosophy". He sets forth a number of implications in his 14 obligations of top management and most of these will be considered in the chapters to follow as we develop the whole concept of Total Quality Management.

The basic aspects of management of TQM are: (1) an organization to implement the total quality management program, (2) Allocation of resources to support the total quality management concept, (3) Training programs for all employees, and (4) Rewards for good quality. The latter two aspects will be discussed in chapters that follow.

The organization must first understand that TQM means changing the philosophy of existing management, the way most employees think, and the reduction of the layers of authority. Many plants today can be likened to a beehive. In a bee hive, we have the queen bee or the manager, we have the worker bees or the employees, and we have the drones, or the layers of the middle and line managers that generally support the queen bee or the manager. This latter group, the layers of middle and line management must be changed and/or reduced for successful utilization of the minds of the workers.

Modern plants should be operated by employees trained to control the process, their understanding of work schedules, their knowledge of how to operate the line efficiently, their know-how of cooperation and team work, and their overall understanding of how a factory works without someone standing over them giving them direct supervision. Of course, management is necessary to establish the requirements, provide the equipment, facilities, etc. The point is that with TQM, people become trained to do their job, to solve their own problems with dispatch, and they become willing and are able to be held accountable for doing the right thing at the right time all the time.

The resources necessary to train personnel have to be based on the level of employees already on board. Those firms that are now planning for the future should be employing personnel that have the basic understanding of the "tools" of TQM. For those firms that do not have that trained person on board, estimates go well over $1000.00 per person to give them the necessary training. As most people know the food industry has not always hired college educated personnel for many positions in the firm. With the existing sophistication already available in many plants, one really cannot rely on untrained personnel to operate the equipment. Most of the training can be on-site, but time must be provided to educate the personnel properly. The in-house trainer probably will have to attend seminars and workshops to understand the basics of TQM. Some firms rely on outside trainers to come on board for the necessary time to train the personnel. This is all well and good provided they do not leave before the trainees have thorough understanding of TQM.

The leader, manager, CEO, or head person must instill in all employees that he or she is the coach. They should lead by example. They should set the tone for the whole operation. The good manager is one that has self esteem, one that takes great pride in the performance of their players, that is, the employees. As someone stated it, the good manager is like a conductor who holds everything together and makes it all happen. The good manager learns to delegate the authority to the worker, but once transferred the worker must be help accountable. However, there are times when the manager must accept full responsibility, such as, in times of crisis, policy making decisions, ceremonies, and certain personnel problems. Good managers desire to belong, to be accepted and liked by all employees. Good managers instill and maintain group performance. Good managers make decisions, call the plays and make certain that the plays are executed. Some characteristics I believe that are important for the leader, that is, the manager are:

Strong personal ethics, high energy level, ability to set priorities, commitment and dedication, courage, motivator, goal-oriented, contagious enthusiasm, cooperator, good listener, creative, patient, desire to grow and build and lead the firm, and have a strong ability and desire to communicate at all levels including the public at large.

The leader should know his or her values, that is, he or she should not be afraid to try, they must learn how to turn disadvantages into advantages, and how to control stress. The leader should thoroughly understand how to give directions on what to do, how to do it, and why it must be done. Most importantly, the good leader or manager makes all employees feel that they belong to the team, the firm, the family and that they are valued members of the firm today and in the future.

Without questions, the rise and fall of TQM is based on the leadership from the owner, CEO, and/or other senior management. The leader must always present a positive attitude and have greater vision for the future. They should leave little doubt or uncertainty about the direction the firm is going. The leader must provide the firm's people with a strategic plan for the future including such information as growth rate, markets, and required quality levels.

A short course in human relations reprinted from Parade Magazine:

The 6 most important words are: "I ADMIT I MADE A MISTAKE"

The 5 most important words are: "YOU DID A GOOD JOB"

The four most important words are: "WHAT IS YOUR OPINION?"

The three most important words are: "IF YOU PLEASE"

The two most important words are: "THANK YOU"

The one most important word is: "WE"

The least important word is: "I"

14 OBLIGATIONS OF TOP MANAGEMENT

by
Dr. W. Edwards Deming

1. Create constancy of purpose towards improving products and services to provide for long-range needs rather than short-term profitability.

2. Adopt the new philosophy by refusing defective materials, and defective workmanship.

3. Cease dependence on mass inspection by requiring statistical evidence of built-in quality in both manufacturing and purchasing functions.

4. Reduce the number of suppliers for the same item by eliminating those that do not qualify with statistical evidence of quality; end the practice of awarding business solely on the basis of price.

5. Search continually for problems in the system to constantly improve processes.

6. Institute modern methods of training of all employees.

7. Focus supervision on helping people do a better job; ensure that immediate action is taken on conditions detrimental to quality.

8. Encourage effective, two-way communication to drive out fear throughout the organization.

9. Break down barriers between departments by encouraging problem solving teamwork.

10. Eliminate use of numerical goals, posters and slogans for the work force, asking for new levels of productivity without providing methods.

11. Use statistical methods for continuing improvement of quality and productivity; eliminate work standards that prescribe numerical quotas.

12. Remove all barriers that inhibit the worker's right to pride of workmanship.

13. Institute a vigorous program for education and retraining to keep up with changes in materials, methods, product design and machinery.

14. Clearly define top management's permanent commitment to quality and productivity and its obligation to implement all of these principles.

LEADERSHIP SUGGESTIONS THAT PAY DIVIDENDS

by
Wilbur A. Gould

1. Set a good example. Employees tend to emulate the boss, so-- make sure you are worth imitating.

2. Call people by their first name. There is nothing as nice as a cheerful work of greeting.

3. Keep people informed. Eliminate the grapevine. When changes are in the offing, let people know

4. Show a genuine interest in everyone. You can learn to like something about almost everyone, if you try.

5. Be thoughtful of the opinions of others. There are 3 sides to every controversy, yours, the other fellows, and the right one.

6. Be alert to give service. What counts most in life is what we do for others.

7. Give credit when credit is due. Everyone wants and needs recognition.

8. Commend an employee for a job well done. Praise in public, criticize in private. Ridicule a man for his mistakes and he will tend to

avoid situations which expose him to the possibility of making another mistake.

9. Let people know your plans. Ask for their suggestions. Let them know that you want them to play a role in the decision process.

10. Emphasize skill, not rules. Keep an open mind about unorthodox solutions. His or her way may be better than your way.

11. Don't give orders, give requests and suggestions.

12. Give your people goals and a sense of direction. They need to know the why's, what's, and how's of the work.

13. Within the limits of your responsibilities, delegate as much as you can.

14. Give every worker a chance to train for promotion.

15. Make all employees feel that they belong and that they are valued members of your team.

CHAPTER 4

People and Team Building

People are the most important asset in a food firm. How they are treated, how they are trained, how we listen to them, how we recognize and reward them, and how we value them have more to do with a firms success than any other single facet of the food business. The old adage of "check your brains at the gate" is gone. Today every food business firm needs the brains, the ideas, the thoughts, the action, the loyalty, the enthusiasm, and the interest of all our employees.

People know more about what is going on in a production area than most supervisors or management. They work in the system and they are attuned to what is going right and what is going wrong. They can be most helpful to the success of the firm if given a voice in the business. It makes them feel like they are a part of the business. They have the feeling that they are owners. They will take great pride in ownership, they become more enthusiastic, and ultimately they become more productive. By listening to them, their suggestions, and their appraisals, much good can be learned for the successful operation of the firm.

Stein in an excellent publication describes the needs of people that lead to the Quality of Work Life (QWL) as follows:

1. Autonomy, that is reasonable freedom of action while on the job.

2. Recognition, that is, being known as an individual and being visible as a contributor by peers and supervisors.

3. Belonging and having shared goals and values.

4. Progress and development and sense of accomplishments.

5. Status or external rewards beyond pay, that is, promotion, rank in position, and other visible benefits.

6. Decent working conditions.

7. Dignity, that is, treated with respect.

8. Involvement and being a part of the team.

These quality of work life lead to motivation, greater productivity, and ultimately to a much more effective work force and organization. People want to grow and become involved in "their" firm.

People can become involved in the business of the firm by working as a member of a Committee, a Work Group, a Task Force, an Operator Group, or part of the Quality Circle. These groups of people should meet together on a regular basis to identify, analyze, and solve problems in their area of work. The size of the group should be kept to a maximum of 12 so that every member of the group can have sufficient time to contribute at each of the weekly meetings. The group works together as a team and inspire each other as they get everyone involved and motivated to prevent problems, reduce errors and improve quality. The group quickly understands that no one of us is as smart as all of us.

Working in the group or as a team prevents isolation and allows individuals to interact. Working independently may lead to frustration and dissatisfaction. Working together as a team builds moral and success and greater performance. Team players or workers gain much satisfaction by helping the team win or be more productive. Teams work for a common goal. They love to celebrate success and, yes teams do keep score and they discuss their problem areas for the good of the team. Teams have that sense of esprit de corps because they belong and they raise their level of self esteem, performance, and loyalty. Most importantly the team strives for continuous improvement. They constantly follow the Deming cycle PDCA, that is, they Plan, they Do (generate numbers or data), they Check or evaluate their results using statistical techniques, and they Act, that is adopt or start the cycle over until they find the solution. PDCA is a fundamental principle of TQM.

Training of all employees in problem solving principles will provide each employee with skills and much needed experience to operate their unit operation to eliminate the variability to control to given levels. The use of problem solving techniques help them to act responsibly and to make improvement as part of their job. The basic training involves the 5W1H, that is, the What, Where, Why, Who, When, and How of any facet of their area of production and quality assurance. The training includes the use of and application of statistics and statistical process control (see Chapter 6).

Management must reward employees for superior performance. Management must recognize talent and praise those that are excelling for the overall good of the firm. Management must be the employees cheerleader, ego builder, champion, and supporter.

Management must communicate the goals, the objectives, and the mission of the firm to all employees. People want to hear, see, and read about the vision and details of the road that lies ahead. They would like to hear a clarion call to action and know the firm stand on quality, marketing plans, along with productivity. They really want to abandon the concept of mediocrity and move forward with gusto to meet the competition head on. Employees want the firm to commit itself and make known to all its future intentions. Employees want to get on the bandwagon and be a part of the firm so that they can see it grow into the next century.

There is an old Chinese proverb that says, "Tell me and I will forget, show me and I may remember, but involve me and I will understand". Total Quality Management, simply stated, means I will help you work more effectively, smarter, and you will be better off because of your knowledge of TQM.

Elbert Hubbard penned the following statement and entitled it:

REMEMBER THIS

"If you work for a man, in Heaven's name Work for him. *** If he pays you wages which supply you bread and butter, work for him; speak well of him; stand by him and stand by the firm he represents. *** If put to a pinch, an ounce of loyalty is worth a pound of cleverness. *** If you must vilify, condemn and eternally disparage — resign your position, and when you are outside, damn to your heart's content, but as long as you are part of the firm do not condemn. *** If you do that, you are loosening the tendrils that are holding you to the firm, and at the first high wind that comes along, you will be uprooted and blown away, and probably will never know the reason why."

By way of summary when dealing with people from a Managers standpoint, I like to think of the 5 "T's", that is,

1. Talk with your employees

2. Train your employees

3. Team your employees

4. Trust your employees

5. Thank your employees

FIGURE 4.1 — The Deming Cycle

PLAN

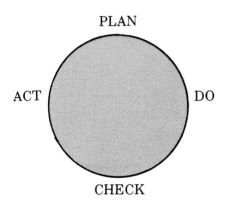

ACT   DO

CHECK

PLAN: Select a project.
            Understand the present situtation, that is,—
            Gather and analyze the facts

DO: Put proposed changes into effect

CHECK: Examine and verify that changes are warranted

ACT: If changes are effective, formalize them
            with appropriate training

CHAPTER 5

Variation

All employees must understand that no two things are exactly alike. Everything varies. People vary, machines vary, operations vary, materials vary, etc. The difference may be only slight, but vary it does. We can usually find and measure physical, chemical, biological differences or variations. Variations in a product are usually due to variations in process.

Having spent some time in the hospital a few years back one can understand variation and why the medical profession needs to know what is normal. For those that have had this experience, you know that the nurse is constantly taking your blood pressure, your temperature, your pulse. They want to know what is normal about you and what is not normal or the amount of variability. They need a picture so that they can study the amount of variation before prescribing medicine or practices.

In a food plant, the same as with man, some variation is common or inherent to the system. These kinds of variation are called common cause of variation. They are variations that the company must resolve if they are committed to quality.

Variability that is unique to the process, one-at-a-time variation is called assignable or special causes of variation. These types of variation relate to the individual process itself and can be resolved by the operator, the supervisor, or the maintenance personnel. However, the employee must have adequate information to solve these kinds of variation. Common causes of variation are small and the expected variation, yet they are stable and predictable. Assignable causes of variation are specific causes that produce normal causes of variation. They are unstable and unpredictable and need to be eliminated.

Some common causes of variation might include the following:
Incoming materials,
Engineering and/or manufacturing assembly,
Operating procedures,
Equipment maintenance,
Environmental conditions,
Process or product design,
Supervisor conditions and /or relationships.

Some special causes of variation might include:
Over adjustments of machines,
Power fluctuations or outages,
Shift to shift operations,
People.

TQM leaders indicate that 80 to 85% of the variation is due to common causes, that is, they are inherent to the system and they stay there until management removes them.

Special causes make up the remaining 15 to 20% of all causes of variation. These kinds of variation are not inherent to the system, but rather they are caused by individual actions or situations. They are easily removed by empowering the operator (employee) to identify the special causes and remove each one one-at-a-time. Thus the operator must be trained and with the control limits to eliminate variability.

Figure 5.1 shows that variation may be caused by Man, Machine, Materials, and/ or by Measurement systems. These are the basic "M's" of the industry. In addition, some people add Environment to the cause of variation. Each of these 4 M's and 1 E are important to understanding the causes of variation and how to go about problem solving.

Perhaps the pictorial designs in Figures 2 and 3 will illustrate these points more specifically and show some of the aspects of variation and concerns to control variation.

FIGURE 5.1 — Causes of Variation

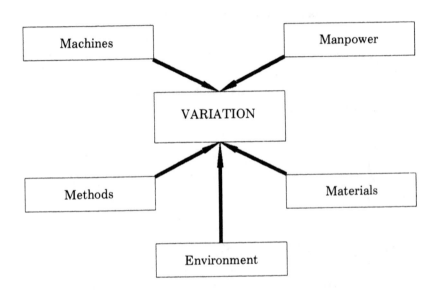

FIGURE 5.2 — Illustration of Sources Of
Variation in a Food Plant

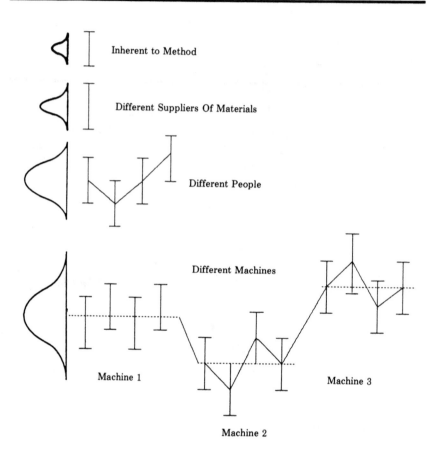

FIGURE 5.3 — Explanation of Sources of
Variation in a Food Plant

PEOPLE

*2nd shift does things differently from 1st shift.
*A trained experienced operator versus an untrained
   inexperienced operator
*Two supervisors disagree about the "best" way to
   run a process
*Poor attitude by some employees-moral is low

MACHINES

*Equipment needs maintenance
*Two machines doing the same job, but set-up
   differently.
*Two different machines operating on the same
   parameters

MATERIAL

*New loads of potatoes, corn, oil, seasoning,
   packaging materials, etc. differing from previous
   loads.
*Stored merchandise deteriorating in storage.

METHODS

*Too much or too little pressure, temperature, time,
   etc.
*Packages not filled or over filled
*Not following FIFO in warehouses
*Product not turned properly in markets
*Handling practices by drivers

CHAPTER 6

Statistical Process Control and Statistical Quality Control

Statistical Quality Control (SQC) is a tool for collecting data and analyzing it after the fact while Statistical Process Control (SPC), some time called just Process Control (PC), is a tool used to collect data during a production run to control the process. These terms have been confusing to some and hopefully, these distinctions will help to better understand the difference.

Using process control tools helps one to make the control impersonal and provides one with an unbiased decision based on observed data. "Statistical Process Control and Statistical Quality Control provides a 2-way flow of information relative the process and those factors which affect it and the quality of the product being manufactured". Statistical Process Control allows employees to control their work.

Henry and Knowles state that "the salesman and the marketing personnel must know the process limitations and be on guard against extravagant and undeliverable claims for the product. At the same time they must be alert to customers needs and the true state of the competition (not rumors) in order to make reasonable requests for improvement and performance and service".

The key to success of any process is facts, therefore, we must learn to collect, analyze, and use data. The facts will provide answers to questions. Of course, the key here is to ask the right questions before generating data. The question (s) must be important and they must be questions that some one cares about.

In any quality improvement program, data is necessary to make the work easier to provide greater assurance of producing products that meet specifications and that are always acceptable.

The first step in generating data is to develop a check sheet, that is, a form to allow entry of numbers from a given phase of the process over time. This kind of data collection is preferred over the simple tabulation of numbers on a data record sheet because in many cases trends can be observed without further analyses.

The ideal data gathering information sheet is the checklist. Checklists are used for start up operations and under actual operating conditions to record any actions taken.. Having been a pilot, one learns quickly to go thru check sheets before take-off.

All data must be accurate and show no bias and be appropriate to the situation. Data, of course, should provide answers to the original question, but data of itself may not solve the problem. That is the reason we have problem solving tools as explained below.

Once we have data, we must properly interpret the numbers. We do this with the aid of statistics. Statistics are the common language that breaks down barriers between levels, departments, and people. The use of statistical information eliminates pointing fingers at people, rather it focuses on corrective actions on the sources of product and process variability. Thus, control of quality is largely the control of variability.

The use of statistics changes the emphasis from detection to prevention. The use of statistical information provides evidence of how the system is performing and the information makes for an effective way to make decisions.

The use of statistical process control becomes the tool for the operator to know when to adjust, when to leave the process alone, when to shut-down the process, and when to seek corrective action (s). The charts and information become the common language of the operator when discussing the output from the process.

Statistical process control will lead to lower costs of production, more uniform levels of quality (less variation from special causes), and a positive way to predict the process capability. In all cases, users of statistical process control state that there is greater productivity and the process is predictable and capable of meeting the customers expectations all the time.

Many firms have already changed from the "old way" to the "new way", that is they have gone from the concept of detection to the concept of prevention. For example, in the old way the product was manufactured, checked, attention focused on how to dispose of it, followed by a detailed emphasis on sampling plans for future 'control'. The modern way is to measure the process while making the product, control the process while in operation, predict the quality of the outcome from processing, and continue to study the process by always looking for ways to improve it.

Some firms have gone much farther and they have changed over from the "old way" to the "new way", that is, in the old way they had many suppliers, vague specifications, inspection before use, and carried large inventories (Just In Case (JIC)). The new way is to use selected suppliers that deliver on time and within given specifications followed by use based on supplier's data and the processor carries a reduced inventory, that is, Just In Time (JIT) for delivery to the customer. Everything is in control, thus, processing labor is reduced, waste is limited, energy is saved, and overall costs are in-line. Thus, the price of quality (POC) is in conformance at all times, that is, the costs are in line to get things done right the first time. In the old way, the price of quality is non-conformance, that is, all the costs of doing things wrong (PONC) or doing them over. In the old way, quality is unpredictable or quality is "what you see is what you get", while in the new way, quality is planned and predictable, that is, "we know what to expect at all times".

Process control is designed to improve product quality. Further, it is a system designed to increase productivity by helping employees work smarter, not harder, through an understanding of the processes or unit operations in the plant. The use of PC provides a tool for the operator to know when to make adjustments or when to take corrective actions or when to leave the process alone.

Process Control is based on the following assumptions:

1. WE accept the responsibility for OUR unit operations or the process we work with. Quality Assurance through evaluation should not have to tell us when to make adjustments in each unit operation within the process. Quality Assurance personnel should help us by working on the system to improve the performance of the process(s).

2. WE share information and ideas fully and we have the complete trust between the operator, the mechanic, the supervisor, and the technologists, etc.

3. WE gain full knowledge of each step in the process; WE know the full capabilities of each unit operation in the process; and, WE know what the requirements are for each unit operation by given products within the system.

4. WE have a continuing awareness of each unit operation in the process and what it must do for control of the product quality. Further, WE are able to react immediately when out-of-order situations develop. Thus, WE are able to prevent problems because we have a thorough knowledge of the unit operations and the system.

5. WE are responsible for our unit operation and WE can be held accoutable for product quality and productivity of the unit operation and/or the process.

THEREFORE, WE have the vision and the capability to perform at optimum efficiency 100% of the time and WE will continuously make measurable improvements with results that are obvious to everyone in the firm.

The following are the basic tools for Total Quality Management used to (1) identify the causes of the problems in the workplace and (2) to control the process within established specification limits. These tools are used to learn how to break the problems down into "bite sized" pieces so that we can work on them to solve quality and productivity problems (SEE PROCESS SYSTEM ANALYSIS flow diagram). Briefly, the "tools" of TQM are the following:

BRAINSTORMING- A tool used to generate all the possible causes of a given selected problem. The session is free-wheeling and no evaluation of the ideas is made. Once the session is over, the ideas are turned over to evaluate the possible causes of any selected problem.

PARETO CHARTING- This is a method by which problems are evaluated by a committe relative their importance. The data is arranged into the "vital few" and "trivial many".

FLOW DIAGRAM- This is a simple step to break down the processing operation (or any other operation, for example handling the office mail) to show the various unit operations of steps in the process for discussion and evaluation.

CAUSE AND EFFECT DIAGRAM- This is commonly referred to as the 'fish-bone' chart, a simple means of breaking down the 4 M's and possible the E into the many components for evaluation by a committee.

Some refer to this diagram as CEDAC, that is, Cause and Effect Diagram and Cards. The individual employees add the cards once the diagram has been laid out and they attach the card to the particular component. This is most valuable as the worker generally knows what is going right or wrong far better than any one individual. The whole idea is to try and get to the real cause of the problem for possible solution.

HISTOGRAM AND FREQUENCY TABLES AND PROBABILITY PLOTS- Once problems are presented, data must be accummulated and then interpreted. A histogram provides a picture of the variations in the process and allows the proper interpretations relative the data as to normal, within specifications, within process control limits, etc. The further calculations to develop the standard deviation (sometimes the range will do), the average, and the specification limits aid the operator to determine the need for change to bring the process back into the specified limits. Generally histograms are only of value on static type data. Frequency tables provide information to show patterns of variation from the data or the distribution of the data. Sometimes the table include the dollar values and the accumulative effects or percentages. If one turns the table 90 degrees, the chart will look like the histogram and show a bell shape to it. The probability plot provides a way to predict product values as to levels of acceptance, rejection etc. based on given tolerances.

CONTROL CHARTS- These are moving pictures of what really is going on with any given unit operation of the process itself. The average and range are calculated from random samples over time and plotted to show possible trends, if any. By using this information and the Upper and Lower Control Limits, the operator knows when to adjust and when to leave the process alone.

CORRELATIONS OR SCATTER DIAGRAMS- These are most useful when one wishes to know the relationship between two variables. It is a device for testing given theories.

After we have learned and practiced the use of the above tools of quality, we need to understand how to Design Experiments (DOE). There are many ways to setup and conduct experiments in a food plant. Careful planning, data taking, and proper analysis will lead to helpful answers to complicated situations. One of the most common practices is the use of analysis of Variance, commonly referred to as ANOVA. This is a statistical technique for analyzing data to show significance between given variables. The analysis is somewhat complicated, but an excellent tool to show interactions among variables that may or may not affect a given product.

The first step in TQM is to find out where we are, that is using a check sheet and generating the numbers by appropriate measurements, followed by analysis and interpretations. Lord Kevin emphasized the relationship between data and learning by noting "when you can measure what you are speaking about and express it with numbers you know something about it; but when you cannot measure it, when you cannot express it with numbers, your knowledge is meagre and unsatisfactory". Thus, data provides information for intelligent discussions, not opinions or emotions.

Next to people, data are the most underutilized resource available to management.

FIGURE 6.1 — The Old Way vs The New Way

THE OLD WAY	THE NEW WAY
Accept all material as delivered.	Establish specifications on all incoming materials and accept only those in compliance.
Employ "grab" sample system.	Use statistical sampling plans and sample accordingly.
Control of product quality by quality control personnel.	All production personnel trained in quality control practices and the application and use of Statistical Process Control (SPC).
Segregation of bad products from good products after processing.	Poor products are not produced because of prevention methods utilized in the manufacturing process.
Make the product, Check it, Focus on Disposition, Decide what to do with it, Concentrate on sample plans for future "control".	Measure the process while making the product, Control the process, Predict the outcome, Continue to study the process always looking for ways to improve it.
Criticizing of employees for poor product quality.	Recognition of employees for any improvements in product quality.
Employees receive little or no training for assigned task.	All employees working in the system are adequately trained for the task.
Employees have no say in the decision process.	Employees have a voice in the decision process.
Employees do what they can under the circumstances.	Employees do their job right because they have the proper direction, tools, knowledge, and the right environment.
Employees work according to the clock with little regard to process efficiency or product quality.	Employees develop pride and enthusiasm for the job and the products they produce.
Process whatever is delivered and evaluate the finished product and find a disposition for whatever the qualities.	Measure the process capabilities and control the process to given specifications with predictions of product quality outcome.

FIGURE 6.1 — The Old Way vs The New Way - Continued

THE OLD WAY	THE NEW WAY
Problems are solved by hit or miss pratice.	Problems are solved by Pareto principle and use of Cause and Effect (CEDAC) charts.
Company receives complaints.	Company recieves compliments.
Products are manufactured by "close enough" syndrome.	Products are manufactured according to specifications and in conformance to label requirments.
Quality is controled subjectively.	Quality is controlled objectively.
Problems are always coming up - uncertain about quality.	Never have to say " I'm sorry" - always certain about quality.
Price of quality is nonconformance - what it costs to do things wrong. (PONC)	Price of quality is conformance at all times - what it costs to get things done right the first time. (POC)
Vendors are unpredictable as to quality, delivery and price.	Vandors are rated on quality, delivery schedules, and price
Management is not seen or available	Management is by walking around (MBWA).
Quality is unpredictable - "what you see is what you get."	Quality is planned and predictable - we know "what you see is what to expect at all times.
Process of Detection.	Process of Prevention.

FIGURE 6.2 — Process Control Analysis

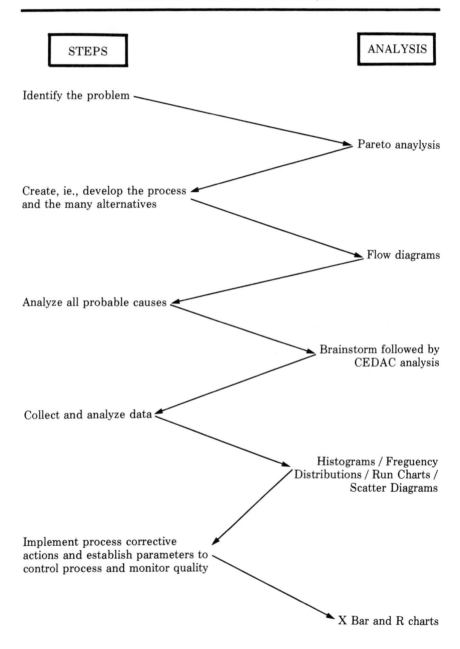

CHAPTER 7

Problem Solving — Brainstorming

(Creation of a "storm" of ideas, that is,
ideas from sudden inspirations)

The concept of Brainstorming was conceived in the "30's" by a man named Alex Osborn, a partner in a New York advertising agency, to generate new ideas for his clients. The idea behind Brainstorming is to gather a group of people together and ask them to create and imagine new ideas individually and collectively as to how to solve a given problem. The old proverb of two heads are better than one really holds true. The participants should be people that have knowledge of the problem and experience in the area. The group should meet in a quiet area free from any distractions and openly exchange ideas and list problems without forming any opinions, theories, or the generation of any data.

There are four basic rules for success with Brainstorming:

1. Create new ideas without judging the merits of the idea, that is, be creative,
2. Emphasize freewheeling, that is, anything goes, the wilder the better,
3. Hitchhiking should be used as it means associating your idea with some one else's, and
4. Try for quantity, that is, get as many ideas as possible.

AN EXAMPLE TOPIC-Why do we have problems with accidents? See Figure 7.1 for some suggestions.

PROCEDURE TO FOLLOW WITH
BRAINSTORMING PROBLEM

1. Identify the problem– written clear description of the problem and the objective on flip chart. One person is designated to record the ideas on the flip chart exactly as they are reported.

2. Select a Leader.

3. Use team approach– get everyone involved with each person offering only one idea in turn.

4. Do not evaluate any idea. Freewheeling, unrelated ideas are OK and should be encouraged. Ideas can come from "hitchhiking" off of some one else's idea.

5. Questions are allowed, but only for clarification of ideas. No one interrupts, censors, or criticizes.

6. People can pass on their turn, but can add ideas on later turns.

7. When everyone passes on a complete turn, the brainstorming session is over.

8. The idea list is turned over to a problem-solving team and they follow-up.

FIGURE 7.1 — Brainstorming

Subject: Why do we have problems with accidents?

1. Negligence
2. Horse play
3. Lack of training in what's right and wrong
4. Unsafe floors
5. Equipment without guards
6. Hot jockeys running forklift trucks
7. No safety clothes
8. No safety goggles
9. No safety gloves
10. Too much lifting required
11. Operations too repetitive
12. Not familiar with assignments
13. Cannot read, speak, or understand English

14. Assigned improper tools
15. In a hurry
16. Family troubles
17. Too tired
18. Lack of coordination for assigned job
19. Not wearing ear plugs, hard hat,etc.
20. Don't like the job.

CHAPTER 8

Problem Solving — Pareto Principle

The Pareto Chart, named for Vilfredo Pareto, is a form of bar chart with each bar representing a cause of a given problem and always arranged so that the most influential cause of a problem can be easily recognized, that is, arranging the problems in descending order. Pareto, a 19th century Italian economist, used this type of analysis to show that the share of wealth was owned by relatively few people--a maldistribution of wealth.

The Pareto principle describes the way causes occur in nature and human behaviour. The Pareto principle tells us that 80% of the problems come from 20% of the causes, based upon actual data collection. The Pareto principle helps to separate the "vital few" from the "trivial many" (Figure 8.1). The Pareto diagram quickly shows us our biggest problems- a very effective communication tool with management for improving the process. The Pareto principle reduces barriers and frustrations, opens doors for more effective communications and focuses personnel's efforts on the problems and solutions that have the greatest potential payback.

Pareto analysis becomes a most effective tool to pinpoint causes of problems, especially by calculating the percentage effects of each cause and adding dollar values. The Pareto philosophy can be used for just about any problem, for example, problems with quality, maintenance time, raw material usage, machine downtime, wasted time, number of jobs that have to be redone, customer inquires, etc.

THE FOLLOWING IS AN EXAMPLE PROBLEM-Where do our complaints come from?

FOLLOW THESE STEPS TO CONSTRUCT
A PARETO DIAGRAM

1. Identify the feature or attribute you are evaluating (i. e. complaints). This will be plotted on the left-hand side or vertical axis.

2. List the types of complaints. Plot these on the bottom or horizontal axis.

3. Make a table of complaint listing the frequency of each complaint in descending order from the highest frequency to the lowest:

EXAMPLE:

Type of Complaint	Frequency
Off flavor	30
Rancid	20
Off Color	10
Poor Texture	8
Too Oily	7
Too Salty	4
Not Enough Salt	3
Too Many Broken-Hash	2
Opening of bag	1
TOTAL COMPLAINTS	85

4. Calculate the frequency of each complaint as a % of the total frequency of complaints.

EXAMPLE:

Complaint Type	Frequency	Frequency %
Off Flavor	30	35.3
Rancid	20	23.5
Off Color	10	11.8
Poor Texture	8	9.4
Too Oily	7	8.2
Too Salty	4	4.7
Not Enough Salt	3	3.5
Too Many Broken	2	2.4
Opening of Bag	1	1.2
TOTAL	85	100

5. Calculate the cumulative frequency % by descending order. For Off-flavor the cumulative frequency % will be the same as the frequency %; however, for defects the cumulative frequency is the sum total of off-flavor and defects, etc.

EXAMPLE:

Defect Type	Frequency	Frequency %	Cumulative Frequency %
Off-Flavor	30	35.3	35.3
Rancid	20	23.5	58.8
Off Color	10	11.8	70.6
Poor Texture	8	9.4	80.0
Too Oily	7	8.2	88.2
Too Salty	4	4.7	92.9
Not Enough Salt	3	3.5	96.4
Too Many Broken	2	2.4	98.8
Opening of Bag	1	1.2	100.0

6. The % frequency for each complaint should be plotted on a chart starting with the greatest complaint to show the magnitude of effect for the "vital few" and "trivial many".

7. A cumulative line may be drawn on the same chart showing the effect of the "vital few" and the small contribution of the "trivial many".

8. The addition of the dollar value ($) is a most significant way to bring the data into clear focus for managements better understanding of the causes of the problem.

PLEASE WORK THIS PROBLEM USING THE FOLLOWING INFORMATION, THAT IS, WHAT ARE THE CAUSES OF ENVIRONMENTAL PROBLEMS IN OUR FACTORY?

Probable causes of environmental problems	Frequency
Too hot	40
Too humid	25
Too much smoke	20
Too much noise	15
Too cold	10
Not enough light	5
Total Complaints	115

FIGURE 8.1 — Pareto Diagram – Consumer Complaints

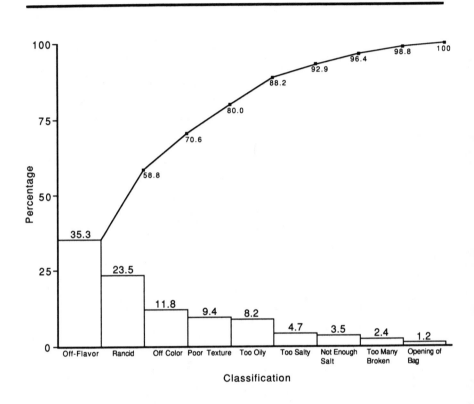

CHAPTER 9

Problem Solving — Frequency Distributions, Histograms, Probability Plots, Specifications, and Capability Index

As stated earlier no two things are exactly alike. Variations exist and things vary according to definite patterns. These patterns are sometimes called frequency distributions. By drawing a line over the points from given measurements we have a frequency distribution curve. The curve tells us a lot about the measurements and more often than not the curve will be bell shaped. The shape of the curve will repeat itself if we continue to take measurements from the same population or lot. Generally the measurements will cluster around the middle or center of the curve and we call this type of curve a normal distribution or curve (See Figure 9.1, 9.2, and 9.3). Other shapes tell us a lot about the data as explained below (See Figure 4).

A histogram is a bar chart showing the variation or distribution of the observations from a set of data. A. M. Guerry in 1833 introduced this problem solving tool in France to show the number of crimes corresponding to various categories of the criminals, such as age. He won the medal of the French Academy for his work and today it is a standard tool for summarizing, analyzing, and displaying data.

A histogram is a simple but powerful tool for elementary analysis of data. When one adds the Frequency Distribution and the Probability Plot information, one can intelligently study the data and draw significant conclusions. As explained earlier, variation is everywhere and the various sets of data will show patterns of the various types of variations or distributions.

The Normal or natural distribution of data is shown in Figure 9.1, 9.2, and 9.3. Other shapes are shown in Figure 9.3 with the Double Peaked Distribution showing us that two sets of processes are at work at the same time, that is, two levels of qualities, two machines, two shifts, etc. The Plateau Distribution often happens as it is an indication of no really defined process or training, that is, everyone does it his or her way. The Comb Distribution probably is due to measurement error. The Skewed Distribution in which the peak is off center often occurs when the specification limit exists on one side or the equipment set point will not function above or below a given set point. The long tail on one side could make for a negative impact on quality with potential customer dissatisfaction. The Truncated Distribution is not desirable and usually is due to some external force which should be removed. The Isolated Peaked Distribution indicates two processes are at work and the Edged Peak Distribution indicates an accurate recording of the data.

A normal distribution is a mathematical model which describes the distribution of many natural and industrial processes. It is based on the assumption that most of the output of a process will be close to the average value with fewer and fewer observations occurring as one departs in either direction from the average. To describe this distribution we need two measurements. One for the central tendency (mean or average) and the other for its dispersion (standard deviation or range, that is, largest value -smallest value). The mean identifies the location of the center of the distribution and the standard deviation (sigma) describes variations from the mean. Also, the standard deviation helps describe the shape of the curve. If the value of the standard deviation is small the bell shape will be narrow. The standard deviation is used to interpret the data as follows, that is, :

± 1 standard Dev. $= 0.68$ or 68% of total area or data

± 2 standard Dev. $= 0.95$ or 95% of total area or data

± 3 standard Dev. $= 0.997$ or 99.7% of total area or data

Plus or minus 3 standard deviations or 6 standard deviations $=$ spread or the best measure of the dispersion (Figures 9.1, 9.2, and 9.3).

The data in Figure 9.5 shows the process capability. This is simply the full range of normal process variation and is usually targeted at the normal value for spread of the process, that is, 6 standard deviations. It tells us what the process is capable of doing.

The specification width or limit may be and should be somewhat larger than the normal spread or process variation. The specification width or limit is set by the customer as their functional requirements. It tells us what characteristics our product must have to meet the customers expectations. The process limits are due to the inherent variation of the process due only to common causes. The process is said to be in control when only the source of variation is from common causes. The relationship of process capability and customer specification is shown in Figure 9.5 and 9.6.

The capability of a process is determined by the total variation that comes from common causes. It may represent as much as 6 standard deviations. The customer may expect much less variation in the products that they buy. Thus, one would conclude that a process that has variations up to 6 standard deviations is not capable of complying with most customer expectations. Therefore, one must know the capability of a process. It is called the CAPABILITY INDEX and is determined by dividing the specification width by the process width. The higher the number, the more capable the process.

Capability Index (CP_k) = Specification Width/Process Width

The capability Index is a most useful measurement of the "health" of a process (see Figure 9.7)

The information in Figure 9.8 shows what continuous improvement can do for a processor. As one notes with continuous improvements, rejects are eliminated, the average is more pointed with the spread much less and, of course, the product is well within specifications.

A Probability Plot is often used to test the capability of the process. It is a method of estimating how well the measurements used to make the average and range chart fit a normal curve. It, also, estimates the shape of the distribution. It is a graph of the cumulative percentages from a frequency table. We use the measurements as shown in the frequency distribution table and take the averages for each range of measurement and plot them in such a way that we can estimate how well they fit a normal curve. It is the best estimate of the machine capability. One must use special graph paper as attached and plot the corresponding frequency versus the actual value. The line connecting the points will indicate at what level the process is meeting expectations. One can calculate the estimate of the standard deviation from a frequency plot by subtracting the largest value from the smallest value and divided by 6.

Frequency Distributions, Histograms, Probability Plots, Specifications, and Capability Index are used to summarize data and to tell a story regarding a process or measurements of product. The histogram is a tool to graphically represent a frequency table. As indicated above, the shape of the curve in the frequency distribution and the histogram and the line in the probability plot can often provide clues to causes of the problems. The Capability Index tells us what the process is capable of doing while the specification width tells us if the process is within specifications, that is, 6 standard deviations.

To construct a Frequency Table and a Histogram, one must first find the highest value and lowest value for the sample. Next one must establish the proper number of class intervals. The following is a rough guide that works:

Observations	Correct number of classes
25-50	6-8
51-100	7-10
101-250	8-12
Over 250	12-20

Next, one must determine the width of the class interval, that is, divide the range of the data by the number of class intervals. Complete the Frequency Distribution Table as follows:

1. Record the measured values by class intervals on the Frequency Table form in the left hand columns.

2. Starting with the lower limit of the class containing the smallest value in the sample and tally the number of values occurring in each class. Record these as tick marks on the form.

3. Draw a curve over the ticks to represent all the values. The curve should be bell shaped if the data is normal. The number of occurrences (frequency) of any given value is represented by the length of the bar. If this form is turned 90 degrees to the left, we have a bell shaped curve similar to the actual histogram of the data.

4. On the right hand side of the Frequency Table tally up the number of occurences for each value and record in the frequency column.

5. Calculate the cumulative frequency by adding each value to each other consecutively and record in the cumulative frequency column.

6. Calculate the cumulative frequency in percent by dividing each of the cumulative frequency values by the total.

7. Calculate the cumulative frequency ascending and descending values. These are most helpful to see where given percentages of the samples fall for any given lot.

8. Calculate the Standard Deviation by using the following formula:

a. Standard deviation (s) = class interval (c) X square root of sum (S) of fd squared/frequency - square of the frequency divided into the sum of fd.

$$ S = C \sqrt{ \frac{Sfd}{f} - \left(\frac{Sfd}{f} \right)^2 } $$

9. One of the most useful uses for the data from the Frequency distribution table is to calculate the Coefficient of Variability by dividing the average into the standard deviation and multiplying by 100. This number is most useful when comparing two runs, two machines, two treatments, etc. The larger the number the greater the difference between the two runs, two machines, two treatments, etc.

If a separate Histogram is to be constructed use the Histogram form and label the vertical axis by starting out at zero on the bottom line and continuing upwards to approximately 25.

On the horizontal axis of the histogram form, skip several lines and fill in the same cell widths as used for the Frequency Table.

Record the actual data and draw horizontal bars to cover the data in each cell. Next draw a curve of best fit over the top of the bars. The curve should take the shape of a bell if the data is normally distributed.

Calculate the average and standard deviation of the data by using the formulas as given on the Frequency Distribution form.

Upper and Lower Specification Lines may be drawn in by using the 6 standard deviation values.

Histograms depend on a truly random sample, a minimum sample size of 50 units. The shape of the curve should accurately reflect the distribution of values in the sample units.

Finally, the Probability Plot should be constructed on the attached Probability Plot form by labeling the vertical axis the same as on the frequency table. Draw in the approximate location of the upper and lower specification limits. Next plot points on your probability plot using cumulative percentage values from your frequency table. If the data appears to be an approximate straight line, draw in the line. The line should tell you the percentage of the lot that will be equal to or less than the specification limit. The curve may not be a straight line if the data is not a normal bell shaped curve. Sometimes just drawing a curve from the assending or descending data under the Cumulative Frequency percent will illustrate the point and these can be interpreted much the same way.

FIGURE 9.1 — A Normal Bell Curve

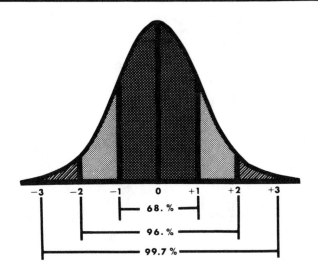

FIGURE 9.2 — Expected Weight Distribution of Product
in Control and Underweight

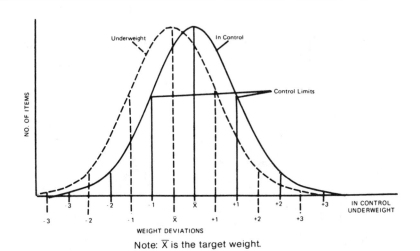

Note: $\overline{X}$ is the target weight.

FIGURE 9.3 — Common Histogram Patterns and Shapes

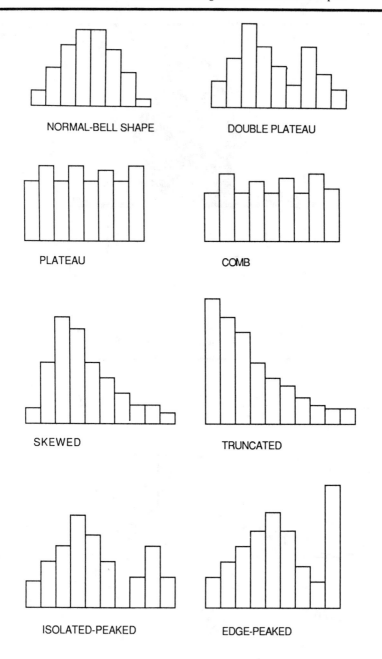

NORMAL-BELL SHAPE   DOUBLE PLATEAU

PLATEAU   COMB

SKEWED   TRUNCATED

ISOLATED-PEAKED   EDGE-PEAKED

FIGURE 9.5 — Understanding Process Capability

A stable process is a process represented by 6 standard deviations (sigma) (6) or ± *3 sigma (6).*
Comparing 6 standard deviations of a process to customer specification provides a measure of the process capability, for example:

Customer specification	= 10 - 30 (20)
Process average or mean	= 20
Process standard deviation	= 2
± 3 standard deviations	= ± 6
10-30 (20)	

The question is, is the process capable of meeting customer specifications?

Since the average is 20, 6 standard deviations =

$$20 - 6 = 14$$
$$20 + 6 = 26$$

Thus,the process is capable of meeting the customers expectations as the spread is 14 to 26 and the customers specification is 10 to 30 or shown graphically as follows:

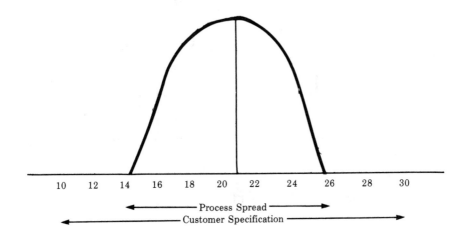

FIGURE 9.6 — Examples of Two Processing Capabilities

1. PROCESSING WITHIN SPECIFICATIONS

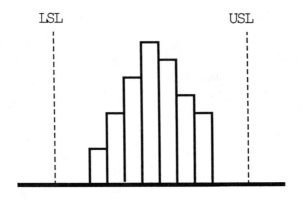

2. PROCESS NEEDS ATTENTIONS

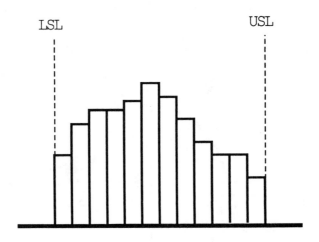

LSL = Lower Specification Limit

USL = Upper Specification Limit

FIGURE 9.7 — Examples of Capability Index, that is,
Cp_K = Specification width/Process width

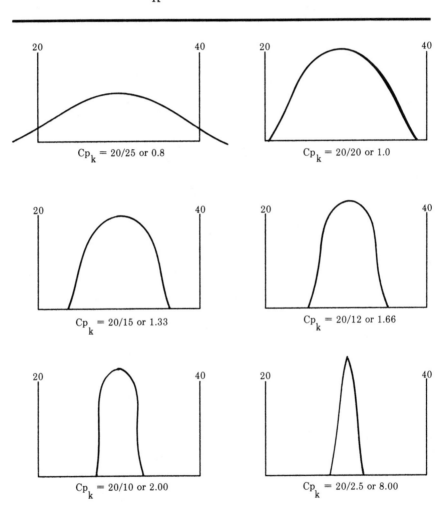

Cp_k = 20/25 or 0.8

Cp_k = 20/20 or 1.0

Cp_k = 20/15 or 1.33

Cp_k = 20/12 or 1.66

Cp_k = 20/10 or 2.00

Cp_k = 20/2.5 or 8.00

FIGURE 9.8 — Statistical Approach to Variability
Vs Engineering Specifications

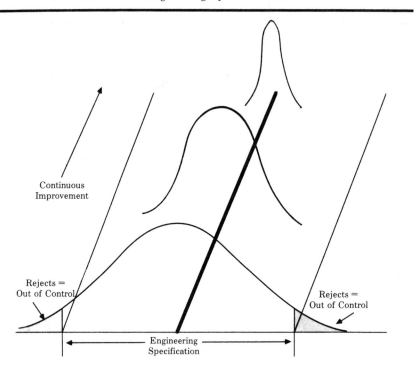

Continuous
Improvement

Rejects =
Out of Control

Rejects =
Out of Control

Engineering
Specification

FIGURE 9.9 — Frequency Distribution for Measured Variable

Class Interval (Value) (c)	Frequency	f	d	fd	fd²	%	Cumulative Frequency in % Ascending	Descending
18	ʃʃʃʃ	1	-4	-4	16	0.5	0.5	100.0
19	ʃʃʃʃ ʃʃʃʃ	10	-3	-30	90	5.0	5.5	99.5
20	ʃʃʃʃ ʃʃʃʃ ʃʃʃʃ ʃʃʃʃ ʃʃʃʃ ʃʃʃʃ 111	33	-2	-66	132	16.5	22.0	94.5
21	ʃʃʃʃ ʃʃʃʃ ʃʃʃʃ ʃʃʃʃ ʃʃʃʃ ʃʃʃʃ ʃʃʃʃ ʃʃʃʃ ʃʃʃʃ ʃʃʃʃ ʃʃʃʃ	55	-1	-55	55	27.5	49.5	78.0
22	ʃʃʃʃ ʃʃʃʃ ʃʃʃʃ ʃʃʃʃ ʃʃʃʃ ʃʃʃʃ 1	31	0	0	0	15.5	65.0	50.5
23	ʃʃʃʃ ʃʃʃʃ ʃʃʃʃ ʃʃʃʃ 11	22	1	22	22	11.0	76.0	35.0
24	ʃʃʃʃ ʃʃʃʃ ʃʃʃʃ 11	17	2	34	68	8.5	84.5	24.0
25	ʃʃʃʃ ʃʃʃʃ 1	11	3	33	99	5.5	90.0	15.5
26	ʃʃʃʃ 111	8	4	32	128	4.0	94.0	10.0
27	ʃʃʃʃ 1	6	5	30	150	3.0	97.0	6.0
28	111	3	6	18	108	1.5	98.5	3.0
29	11	2	7	14	98	1.0	99.5	1.5
30	1	1	8	8	64	0.5	100.0	0.5
	S (Total)	200		36	1030	100.0		

Z = 22

1. Standard Deviation (68%): $s = c\sqrt{\dfrac{Sfd^2}{f} - \left(\dfrac{Sfd}{f}\right)^2}$

$= 1\sqrt{\dfrac{1030}{200} - \left(\dfrac{36}{200}\right)^2} = \sqrt{5.15 - 0.0324} = \sqrt{5.1176} = 2.26$

2. Standard Deviation (95%): $2s = 4.52$

3. Standard Deviation (99%): $3s = 6.78$

$\overline{X}$ (Average) $= Z + \dfrac{c \times Sfd}{Sf} = 22 + \dfrac{1 \times 36}{200} = 22 + 0.18 = 22.18$

CV (Coefficient of Variability) $= \dfrac{s}{\overline{X}} \times 100 = \dfrac{2.26}{22.18} \times 100 = 0.102 \times 100 = 10.2\%$

FIGURE 9.10 — Variable Data Form

VARIABLE DATA FORM   DATE:

CHARASTERISTIC: _   **TECHNOLOGIST:**

UPPER SPECIFICATION LIMIT   LOWER SPECIFICATION LIMIT

TARGET   RANGE   COEFFICIENT OF VARIABILITY:

Observation	Value	Observation	Value	Observation	Value	Observation	Value	Observation	Value
1	26	21	24	41	29	61	21	81	23
2	20	22	27	42	30	62	20	82	24
3	23	23	26	43	26	63	22	83	26
4	21	24	25	44	25	64	21	84	27
5	19	25	24	45	26	65	24	85	26
6	20	26	25	46	24	66	23	86	27
7	20	27	23	47	24	67	27	87	24
8	22	28	20	48	23	68	28	88	23
9	24	29	21	49	27	69	27	89	22
10	19	30	22	50	22	70	26	90	21
11	23	31	24	51	23	71	29	91	22
12	24	32	26	52	20	72	21	92	20
13	22	33	22	53	20	73	23	93	21
14	20	34	28	54	21	74	23	94	23
15	21	35	24	55	19	75	22	95	24
16	23	36	26	56	22	76	21	96	26
17	20	37	21	57	23	77	20	97	24
18	19	38	23	58	24	78	24	98	22
19	26	39	27	59	25	79	24	99	21
20	25	40	28	60	22	80	25	100	22

average	23.37
stand. dev.	2.58
max. value	30.00
min. value	19.00

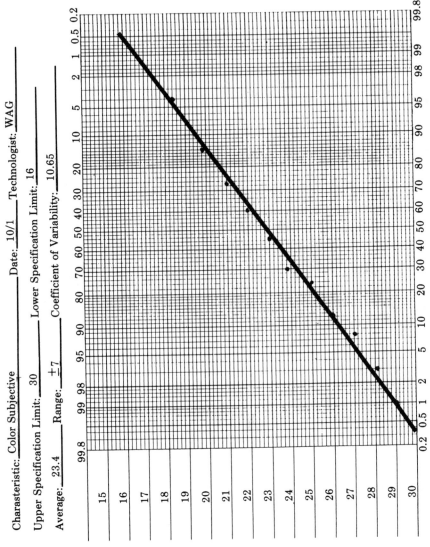

FIGURE 9.11 — Normal Probability Plot Form

Charasteristic: Color Subjective _____ Date: 10/1 ___ Technologist: WAG _____

Upper Specification Limit: 30 _____ Lower Specification Limit: 16 _____

Average: 23.4 ___ Range: +7 ___ Coefficient of Variability: 10.65 _____

CHAPTER 10

Problem Solving — Process Flow Chart or Diagram and Quality Assurance – Critical Control Point Indentification

The Process Flow Diagram visually shows how an item or product moves through a system and WHO or WHAT acts upon or interacts with it, that is, the events that occur. It is a picture of the process. A Process Flow Diagram reveals the different perceptions about the process and the unrecorded changes in a given system. A Process Flow Diagram should show the various critical control points that have an impact on the final quality. Figure 10.1 shows a generic process/ product improvement model (taken from Burr, Quality Progress 6/90).

The advantages of a Process Flow Diagram is that everyone can see the process rather than just each verbalizing about it. Secondly, one can see the interdependencies of the various steps in the process. Thirdly, all the information can be put on one page for guidance of all concerned.

The Process Flow Chart should be a simple step by step running account of what is really happening in the process. Some people use symbols like a square to indicate inspection, a circle to indicate an operation, a half circle to indicate delay, a triangle to indicate storage, and an arrow to indicate transportation (See Figure 10.2). Regardless of the construction of the process flow diagram, each function or unit operation should be identified. Secondly, all critical control points that have an effect on quality should be identified independently at the side of the unit operation. These critical control points or functions usually end with an "ing" suffix and they are most helpful in describing the activity. Thirdly, from a process stand point, all parameters of operation should be enumerated with upper and lower specification limits attached.

The key to any process flow chart or diagram for solving problems is to complete a critical control point/corrective action form as indicated in Figure 10.3. This form should be approved by the Product Manager, the Production Manager, the Quality Control Manager, and the Plant Manager along with the responsible person for each of the jobs or unit operations. No form is of any value unless the needed action is followed through to completion. Management should assign a person to follow through on each approved corrective action project.

The Process Flow Chart or Diagram is used to Identify individual events that occur in a process, such as, What can be done about hash in our products?

First, one should draw a flow chart for your operation or a given operation (see example for potato chips) and identify all the critical control points that have an effect on hash.

Persons that work on the process should make the flow chart, however, all members of the team should participate and ask the basic questions (5W1H):

Where does the material, service, for each unit operation etc. come from?
How does the material go through the process?
Who makes the decision(s) to change the process?
What happens if the finished product is not acceptable?
Why are the specifications not adhered to?
When are changes made in the parameters of each unit operation?

Other questions should be asked, but the questions should not offend any participant by putting them on the defense.

The benefits of flow charting can be summarized as follows:
    1. The people who work on the process become more familiar
    with the whole operation.

2. Improvements can be made easier.

3. Greater communications develop after studying the flow chart.

4. The employees become more enthusiastic supporters of quality efforts when they see the big picture and the total effort in the manufacture of the product.

5. Everyone has a better understanding of the process and the various factors that can and do affect quality, waste, and productivity.

Another advantage of the Process Flow Chart is everyone can start evaluating the problem areas through the use of the Critical Control Point/Corrective Action form by selecting the top critical control points as a group and ranking them from most critical to least critical by vote of the group. A Pareto Chart is the ideal way to bring these critical control points into focus, particularly when the dollar values are added. The data will quickly point up the "vital few" and the "trivial many" causes of the problem, in this case, hash in the finished product.

See Figures 10.1, thru 10.5 on pages 68-72.

FIGURE 10.1 — Flow Charting Symbols

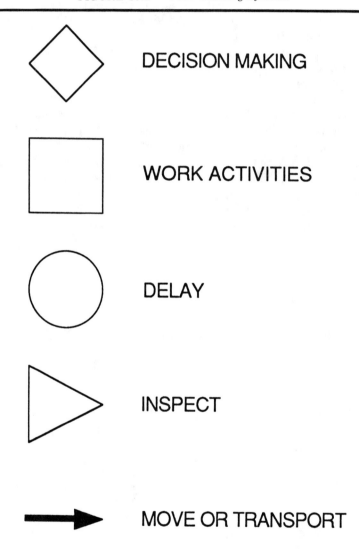

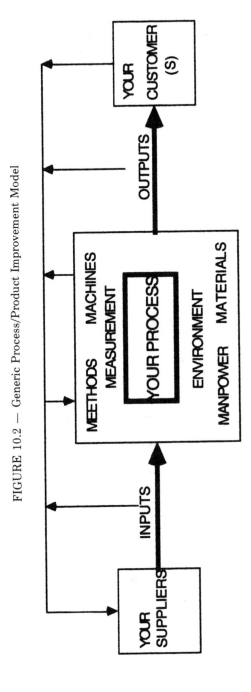

FIGURE 10.2 — Generic Process/Product Improvement Model

Models are used to Define, Measure, Improve, Control, Assess, Design, Cost, Conform, and/or Establish Requirements and Specifications to meet customers expectations

FIGURE 10.3 — Critical Control Point/Corrective Action Form

Plant:_____Date:_____

Critical Control Point No.:_____Revision Date:_____

Unit Operation:_____

Critical Control Point:_____

Operation Task:_____

_____

_____

Responsibility:_____

Reason for Control:_____

_____

Method of Control:_____

_____

Operating Procedure:_____

_____

_____

Corrective Action:_____

_____

Review Procedure:_____

_____

Developed by:_____Date:_____

PRODUCT MGR.　　PRODUCTION MGR.　　QA MANAGER　　PLANT MGR.

FIGURE 10.4 — Potato Chip Manufacture & Distribution
with Quality Assurance Check Points

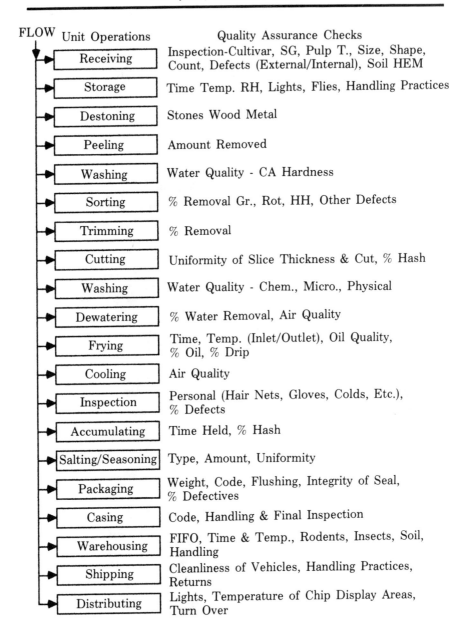

FLOW Unit Operations	Quality Assurance Checks
Receiving	Inspection-Cultivar, SG, Pulp T., Size, Shape, Count, Defects (External/Internal), Soil HEM
Storage	Time Temp. RH, Lights, Flies, Handling Practices
Destoning	Stones Wood Metal
Peeling	Amount Removed
Washing	Water Quality - CA Hardness
Sorting	% Removal Gr., Rot, HH, Other Defects
Trimming	% Removal
Cutting	Uniformity of Slice Thickness & Cut, % Hash
Washing	Water Quality - Chem., Micro., Physical
Dewatering	% Water Removal, Air Quality
Frying	Time, Temp. (Inlet/Outlet), Oil Quality, % Oil, % Drip
Cooling	Air Quality
Inspection	Personal (Hair Nets, Gloves, Colds, Etc.), % Defects
Accumulating	Time Held, % Hash
Salting/Seasoning	Type, Amount, Uniformity
Packaging	Weight, Code, Flushing, Integrity of Seal, % Defectives
Casing	Code, Handling & Final Inspection
Warehousing	FIFO, Time & Temp., Rodents, Insects, Soil, Handling
Shipping	Cleanliness of Vehicles, Handling Practices, Returns
Distributing	Lights, Temperature of Chip Display Areas, Turn Over

FIGURE 10.5 — Some Critical Areas for Accumulating Hash in Potato Chips

1. Size and shape of the raw potato

2. % percent removal of slivers etc. following slicing

3. Slice thickness

4. Uniformity of slicing

5. Handling of the chips after frying

6. Handling the chips in the accumulating system

7. Handling the chips with the conveying systems

8. Handling the chips thru the packaging systems

9. Casing chips

10. Handling the chips into and out of warehouse

11. Handling the chips thru the marketing system by the route salesman and the supermarket clerks

12. Handling the chips by the customer and in the home

CHAPTER 11

Problem Solving —
Cause and Effect Diagram

Cause and Effect Charting (CEDAC) is a simple technique for dissecting a problem or a process. Cause and Effect Chart is, also, known as the Ishikawa Chart as developed by Kaoru Ishikawa in 1942 while at the University of Tokyo. It is, also, sometimes referred to as the Fishbone Chart or the 4M's and E Chart.

CEDAC identifies all possible relationships among INPUT AND OUTPUT Variables, that is, the five categories on the following skeleton (Fishbone) (Materials, Machines, Man (workers), Methods, (Measurements may be added) and Environment. The potential contributing causes are then drawn as ribs off of the main branches.

CEDAC organizes the thinking and provides a plan of attack all at the same time. Further, CEDAC brings out all known factors (causes), not just the suspected ones. This is accomplished by using cards to help explain in short sentences the details of the cause. In the real world, employees using CEDAC write out their observation, their ideas, and their know how on a 3 X 5 card and place these cards on the diagram in the appropriate place. This information is then available to anyone to see, to study, and to add to with another card. Thus, the main purpose of CEDAC is to classify the various causes using the information that is available and thought to have an effect on the cause to help arrive at a quantitative answer.

CEDAC may be used to (1) analyze a process, (2) to solve problems (and (3) to make improvements. CEDAC is an effective communication mechanism. One way to use CEDAC is to follow these suggested steps:

1. Form a team of persons concerned about a problem. In our case, the problem is the lowering of accidents in the food plant.

2. List all the various problem areas (causes) on the "Fishbone" diagram under the 4M's and E. Start by writing in the description of the problem, that is the effect. In the real World, the diagram should be hung on a wall and employees are asked for their contributions to solving the problem (see 5 below).

3. The group should brainstorm all the major causes which contribute to the effect and write them in at the end of one of the branches or bones which point to the main backbone or line.

4. Write in all the sub-factors which may contribute to the major factors as small branches off the appropriate branch.

5. In the real World, ask all the employees to write in any ideas which they may have to solve the accident problem by filling out 3 X 5 cards and pining them to the appropriate branch. Determine all the capabilities of solving the problem using actual accident data. (Normally followed up by using statistical methods).

6. Analyze the data by brainstorming each of the ideas and rank these according to the Pareto Principle to arrive at the "vital few" and the "trivial many". Generate actual data from the reports and interpret your data and theorize as to the possible solutions.

7. Implement suggested solutions and install controls using X Bar and R Charting of results.

FIGURE 11.1 is an example of the basic structure of Cause and Effect Diagram which can be used to solve problems. This model shows the inputs from the suppliers and the M's of the industry along with the Environment (People may be substituted for Manpower) with the outputs being the customers. Any one of these inputs may have a direct bearing on the output in terms of quality, productivity, and/or the bottom line.

FIGURE 11.1 — Cause and Effect Diagram

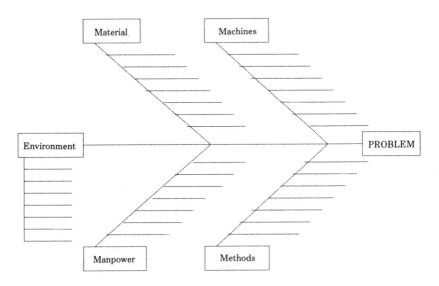

FIGURE 11.2 is one way to illustrate the various causes of problems and their effect on quality, quantity, etc.

FIGURE 11.2 — Cause and Effect Diagram – (Fishbone) - CEDAC

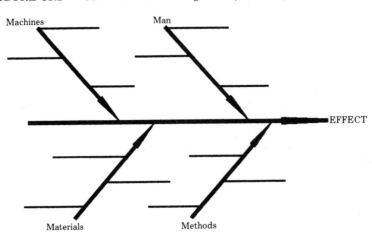

FIGURE 11.3 takes the same Cause and Effect Chart and applies this to Potato Chip Manufacture. This Figure does not break down each of the main causes, such as, for potatoes one of the main materials into the many causes of quality. For example, on side branches of potatoes one could have size, shape, defects, maturity, specific gravity, sucrose, reducing sugars, pesticide residues etc.

FIGURE 11.3 — Example of CEDAC for Potato Chip Manufacture

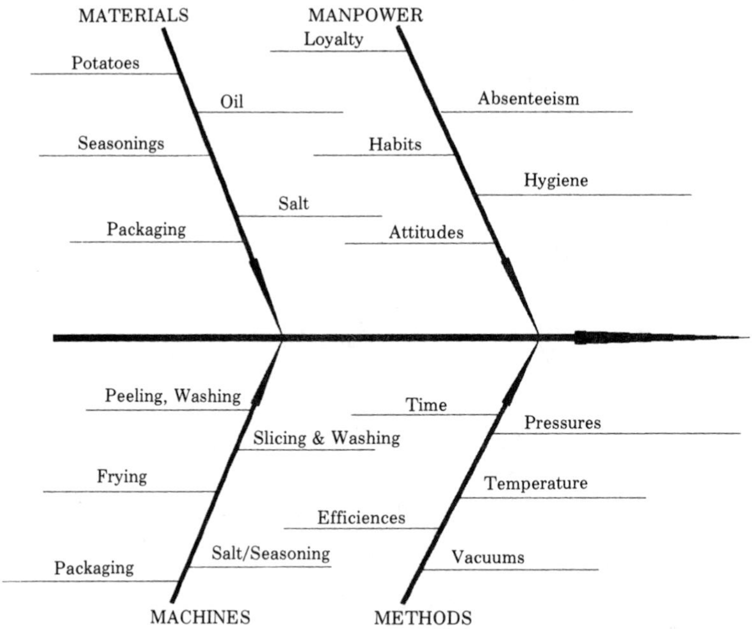

The Concept of CEDAC can be a very valuable tool to most firms. It is simple, helpful, and easy to focus as to the cause of many problems. Some additional benefits of CEDAC include the organizing of all related factors, the involvement of all employees in making an in-depth analysis in solving a problem, and the enjoyment of working together as a team.

CEDAC, of course, is not a complete answer to solving the causes of most problems. It is an important step and it must be followed up with actual data gathering and proper interpretation.

Using the attached Cause and Effect Diagram, How can we improve the flavor of our product (s)? List all the possible causes and wherever possible write out your specific details of the causes.

CHAPTER 12

Problem Solving — Variable and Attribute Charting or X Bar and R Bar Chart Development

Control charts are tools used to study the variation in a repetitive process. They are literally a stretched out histogram. They provide an effective means of continuously monitoring a repetitive process. Control charts tell us what the process is doing now and what it will do tomorrow. Control charts are the actual process talking. They provide a picture of what is really happening. They provide common language for discussing process performance. They give the operator a tool to control the on-going process. They tell us how to distinguish special causes from common causes of variation. They tell us if the process is within or out of specifications. Control charts are used to maintain process performance consistently, predictably, uniformly, and they help reduce costs.

The specification limits are the normal permissible variations that have been established to assure us that the product or process is in conformity or in control. They tell us that the problems are caused by common causes or special causes. Common causes are the faults of the system, representing some 85% of the problems and they are the responsibility of management to improve. The special causes are assignable to chance, that is, materials, machines, methods, man, or the environment causing the problem. These problems can be tracked down and they should be eliminated. They represent some 15% of the problems and are the responsibilities of the operator to correct.

The operator should learn how to read the control chart, that is, X Bar (Average) and R (Range) Charts. If there is a problem, the operator should study the R chart first as it is more sensitive to variations. If the R chart is in control, the operator should then study the X Bar chart to obtain information as to the operating level of the process, machine, etc. The X Bar data will change with Materials, Environment, etc.

Key interpretations include:

Natural pattern is when most of the points are near the central or average line. Some of the points may approach the control limits, but none are outside the control limits. The process is considered stable and predictable.

Outliers are points outside the control limits and may be due to error in measurements. If outliers are present, there should be a search for the cause.

Two-out-of-three rule is where 2 out of 3 successive points are too near a control limit. This is unnatural, hence a special cause exists and it should be investigated with appropriate adjustments made to bring the process into control.

A run of 5 or 6 points means that a trend has been established. If the run is in one direction for 5 or 6 points, an investigation must be made as something is causing this and it is unnatural.

Seven (7) successive points on one side of the line is, also, unnatural and should be investigated.

Points cycling around the average line are significant because normally the points should be randomly distributed about the average. This may be due to machines operating improperly (voltage, bar weight, material variation or some other unnatural cause.)

Several points outside the specification widths or the Upper and Lower Control limits (see below) warrants immediate attention as something has gone wrong.

Sudden change in points may be due to changes in materials, events in the process, or new operator in charge. They should be investigated and the cause should be established.

In addition to the Average and Range, the operator must learn how to calculate and use the upper and lower control limits, UCL for X Bar and R and LCL for the X Bar. (See Figure 12.1 and 12.2).

Some users of the X Bar and R Chart use what is known as the Zone Chart System. They divide the areas between the control limits into three areas, generally using 1 standard deviation for area 1-that is, the Green area meaning the process should be stopped and proper adjustments made to bring the process back into control. Only 1 point in 300 should be in this zone. This caution area means watch carefully and continue to resample until the process is operating within acceptable limits. Zone 3 is the Red Zone and represents 3 standard deviations. Two-thirds of all the points should be in this zone. The Red area simply means continue to operate and leave the process alone as all is OK.

There are several types of control charts as depicted in Figure 12.3 Variable data is the most common and used for controlling measured data. Attribute Charting is used for various types of defects, primarily by counting the number of nonconforming units or the nonconformities per units, that is, acceptable-unacceptable, "go" vs "no go", "yes" vs "no", "pass" vs "fail". The most commonly used attribute control chart is the "p" chart or the percentage of defective items. For example, the number of deffective units are counted and divided by the sample size and multiplyed by 100 to get percent. Thus, 7 defective pieces out of $100 = 7\%$.

The "np" chart is used to monitor the number of defective units. The "c"-chart is used to monitor the number of defects on an item and "u" chart is used to monitor the number of defects on various items. These charts can easily be remembered by thinking of the letters, that is, "p" stands for percentage of defective units, "c" means count or number of units, "np" means number of defective units, and "u" is for number of unlimited defects in variable sample size.

FURTHER DETAILS FOR ATTRIBUTE CHART AND CHARTING ARE FOUND IN THE REFERENCES.

PROBLEM – WHY DO WE HAVE A WIDE VARIATION IN OUR FILL WEIGHT? Obviously to answer this question, one must have data or facts over time. Normally, if using more than one filling machine one would generate the following data for each machine over time. If only one filling machine, the samples should be taken consecutively from each filler head while in operation over time, etc.

Using the attached data, calculate the average (X Bar) and range (R) for the 50 fill weight readings. (Five readings were taken every hour from one machine over a ten-hour period. This could have been set-up to take 5 readings per hour from 10 machines).

Calculate the Grand Average (X double Bar), and the Average for the Range (R Bar).

Plot your data on the X Bar Chart for the average of the readings per hour, in other words 1 value each hour on the line (some people like to plot each weight in the cells and plot the average each hour on the line. I feel this clutters the chart and the Range will tell me this information).

Plot the average for the run (X double Bar) on the X Bar Chart. This normally is the center of the chart and if everything is normal with your machines, your hourly readings will randomly be dispersed around this average line, that is, an equal number either side with no indicated trends or runs.

Next plot the Upper and Lower Control Limits. These are calculated from your data and the statistic for 5 samples (if using more or less than 5 samples, refer to attached table for correct multipliers for A sub 2 and D sub 4).

Now plot the Range (R) values on the R Bar Chart. Again plot the average only and plot it on the hourly line.

Plot the Average of the Range values (R Bar).

Lastly, calculate the Upper Control Limit for the Range using the D sub 4 value in the Attached Table. There is no Lower Control Limit for the Range as it is zero.

You are now ready to interpret your chart using the above information. In the real World, the operator has first hand knowledge of what is happening and can make appropriate adjustments as time progresses when he or she learns to use the charted data.

FIGURE 12.1 — Control Charts to Show Upper and Lower
Control Limits and Process Average and Range

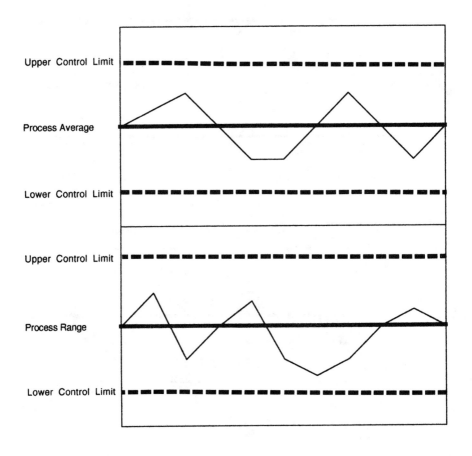

FIGURE 12.2a — Control Chart Illustrating In-Control Situation

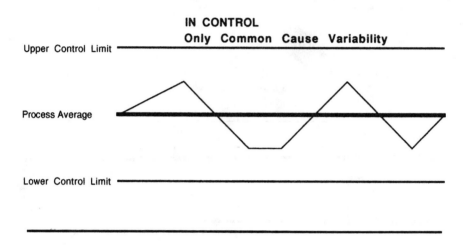

FIGURE 12.2b — Control Chart Illustrating Out-of-Control Situation

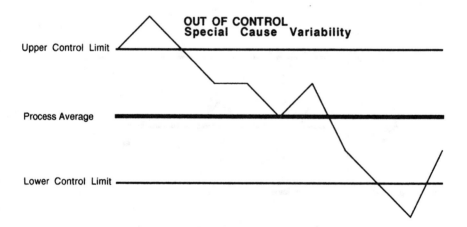

FIGURE 12.3 — Types of Control Charts

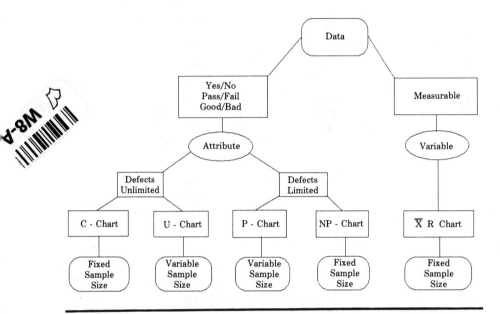

FIGURE 12.4 — Factors for Computing Control Limits

FACTORS FOR COMPUTING CONTROL LIMITS

Number of Readings in Each Subgroup	Chart for Averages A_2	Chart for Ranges		Estimating O from R d_2
		D_3	D_4	
2	1.800	0	3.268	1.128
3	1.023	0	2.574	1.693
4	.729	0	2.282	2.059
5	.577	0	2.114	2.326
6	.483	0	2.004	2.534
7	.419	0.076	1.924	2.704
8	.373	0.136	1.864	2.847
9	.337	0.184	1.816	2.970
10	.308	0.223	1.777	3.078
11	.285	0.256	1.744	3.173
12	.266	0.284	1.717	3.258
13	.249	0.308	1.692	3.336
14	.235	0.329	1.671	3.407
15	.233	0.348	1.652	3.472

FIGURE 12.5 — Average (X Bar) and Range (R) Data Form (Blank)

Product:_____Container   Size:_____Code:_____Plant:_____

Sample   Frequency of Sample Sets   Date:_____   Shift:____Line No:____

No.	1	2	3	4	5	6	7	8	9	10	$\overline{\overline{X}}$	$\overline{R}$
1												
2												
3												
4												
5												
Sum												
Ave.												
XBar												
Range												

Note 1:   Upper Control Limit for Average $(UCL_{\overline{X}}) = \overline{\overline{X}} + A_2\overline{R}$
               Lower Control Limit for Average $(LCL_{\overline{X}}) = \overline{\overline{X}} - A_2\overline{R}$
               Upper Control Limit for Range $(UCL_R) = D_2\ \overline{R}$
Note 2: A_2 for five (5) sample numbers in a set is equal to 0.58 AND D for five (5) sample numbers in a set is equal to 2.11

X BAR CHART

RANGE CHART

FIGURE 12.6 — Average (X Bar) and Range (R) Data Form (Complete)

Product: Potato Chips _____Container   Size: 16 oz. Code: 02072 Plant: WAGCO__

Sample   Frequency of Sample Sets   Date:_____ Shift:_____Line No:_____

No.	1	2	3	4	5	6	7	8	9	10	$\overline{\overline{X}}$	$\overline{R}$
1	18.5	15.2	16.3	19.1	18.7	15.9	16.8	16.0	16.0	16.1		
2	17.0	15.3	14.8	18.4	18.3	15.2	15.8	16.1	16.2	16.0		
3	16.5	18.4	14.6	18.6	17.7	14.8	16.4	16.3	16.5	16.0		
4	16.8	15.0	15.1	16.1	16.2	14.1	15.8	16.0	16.1	16.1		
5	15.0	15.0	15.0	17.5	17.9	15.4	14.9	16.2	16.0	16.2		
Sum	83.8	78.9	75.8	89.7	88.8	75.4	79.7	80.6	80.8	80.4		
Ave. X Bar	16.8	15.8	15.2	17.9	17.8	15.1	15.9	16.1	16.2	16.1	16.29	
Range	3.5	3.4	1.7	3.0	2.5	1.8	1.9	0.3	0.5	0.2		1.88

Note 1:   Upper Control Limit for Average (UCL $\overline{X}$)= $\overline{X}$ + $A_2 \overline{R}$
Lower Control Limit for Average (LCL $\overline{X}$)= $\overline{X}$ - $A_2 \overline{R}$
Upper Control Limit for Range (UCL$_R$)=D_4 $\overline{R}$
Note 2: A_2 for five (5) sample numbers in a set is equal to 0.58 AND D for five (5) sample numbers in a set is equal to 2.11

X BAR CHART

RANGE CHART

CHAPTER 13

Problem Solving — Correlation Charting or Scatter Diagrams

Correlation charting or as sometimes referred to as scatter diagraming is a tool to study how different variables relate to each other or how they correlate. They are used to test for possible cause and effect relationships.

The control variable (cause) should be the bottom or "X" axis (horizontal) of the graph and the measured variable (effect) should be the vertical or "Y" axis on the left side of the chart. The scale should be appropriate to handle all the data and use up at least two/thirds of the graph paper (8 ½ X 11").

Whatever the problem, collect 50 to 100 pairs of samples of the data that you wish to correlate. These data should be plotted on the chart and they should increase in value on both the horizontal and vertical axis.

The completed graph should show a pattern, that is a scatter diagram of the relationships between the two variables.

The relationship of the data may be understood by drawing a line of best fit through the scatter plots. If the scatter plots are all on the line, we say this is a perfect linear correlation. However, if the points are widely scattered, we call this a weak correlation or no correlation. A correlation may be positive if the two measured variables increase together. If one increases and the other decreases, this is a negative correlation. Examples of some correlations are shown in Figure 13.1

FIGURE 13.1 — Some Patterns Showing Types of Correlations

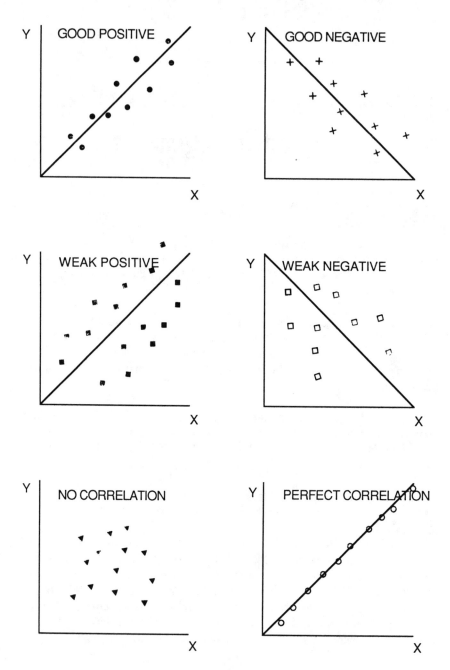

Most PC programs will calculate the statistical significance of sets of data and indicate the degree of correlation. Generally, a correlation of 0.7 would be significant, but it only means that 49% of the data on the "Y" axis are related to the data on the "X" axis. Most users of the correlation want a minimum of 0.8 correlation and that means that 64% of the data on the "Y" axis is related to the data on the "X" axis.

CHAPTER 14

Design of Experiments

All food companies conduct experiments in their plants and laboratories to evaluate new ingredients and materials, new equipment and process, quality assurance methods, development of new products, and other practices to improve productivity and the assurance of quality. In many cases they are most successful, however, in other cases a lot of money is spent with few benefits.

Boss Kettering once stated that "if you wait to do research until you have to, its too late". Many firms make honest efforts to conduct research, but may not understand that research is a science unto itself. It takes money, qualified researchers and the careful design of experiments, followed by proper interpretation of the results. The benefits far outweigh the costs if the research is conducted properly.

Without question production agriculture is far ahead of the food processing industry in research know how. R. A. Fisher, a British scientist, back in the early teens inititated the concept of replication when running experiments to control variability in his crop research. This is the first concept that must be carefully understood today when conducting experiments in our food operations.

Statistically designed experiments will help firms stay competitive and apply rapid and continuous improvement in all aspects of new technology. Effective progress requires effective decision making at all levels. Effective decision making requires an understanding of the current situation and the likely results of the alternatives under consideration. This in turn, requires information. Information comes in two forms: Theoretical understanding of underlying issues and empirical understanding based on observations of how nature works.

Statistical Process Control (SPC) is valuable precisely because it is a systematic means of capturing and building on information that nature is already making available to us. SPC is concerned with the passive acquisition of knowledge. But many times the information is not already available, for example, new processes, new products, new ingredients, new measurements, new equipment, etc. In many other situations the problem is not newness, but unavailability; nature does not want to yield its secrets. Indeed this is often the case in practical troubleshooting or process optimization situations. SPC might reveal that a problem exists and even show where, when, and how it occurs; but still no one can seem to find out why and what to do about it. On the other hand, there might be a need to improve, but so many interacting factors or alternatives affect the situation that it seems to be an over-whelming task to figure out a simple, economic, and safe course of action. Thus it is necessary to design experiments (DOE) to make a planned change, determine the effect of the changes, and to use this information to determine how nature works.

Experiments are used to discover something not known, that is, induce a response from nature. It is from the control over the actions initiated and the assumed casual relationship of the response to this action that the power of the experimental (scientific) method derives success and produces results to solve problems. The scientific method is an orderly system of searching for the truth. Most people agree that there are six steps to be followed when conducting experiments:

1. Identify the problem and establish the objectives and goals of the contemplated study, that is all the why's.

2. All research must start in the library, that is, we must know all that has been done to date.

3. Design the approach to the problem using full randomization procedures, that is, the experimental design must include randomized replications, clear cut and specific procedures, and well defined methods and measurement tools.

4. Gather or collect the data or get the empirical facts, that is, work the proposed plan by recording the facts.

5. Accept or reject the hypothesis based on Least Significant Difference (confidence level at 0.05). In other words answer each objective by interpreting the generated data.

6. Summarize the results, draw conclusions, and make recommendations based on the facts.

Some examples or specific design of experiments follow:

One Variable at a Time (OVAT) Experimentation

The simplest, and probably the most frequent, example of an experiment is manipulation of a single factor to see what effect it has on a response of interest. The factor might be descrete (like different raw material suppliers) or different people or different machines in a manufacturing process. In other cases, the factor might be continuous-capable of assuming any value over a wide range of conditions, that is, temperature, pressure, concentration, etc. At any rate one must collect data (measurements) over time to determine variations under all conditions. The data may be plotted or charted on a graph to get an idea of predictable response for any given value. However, in industry more often than not interactions are most common and one cannot look at one variable at a time. Further, OVAT experimentation effectively denies the existence of interactions and may lead to erroneous conclusions.

Two Factor Interactions (2FI's)

The most common and useful interactions are two-factor interactions (2FI's for short). This would be typical when studying the effect of temperature changes on the color of potato chips from two fryers. One should design the experiment to collect color data from each fryer at given frying temperatures. The collected data might be plotted showing that color was similar from each fryer at any given temperature; however, more likely than not the data would assume drastic difference and could best be shown by plotting the data. Since the temperature effects were continuous, one would expect the color data to be curvature from each fryer, indicating interaction.

The kind of experimentation allows one to analyze the whole system, that is, look at the effect of experimental factor(s) on response(s) of interest simultaneously. First one can determine whether there exists any effect due to the experimental factor(s) on the observed outcome system at a high level of confidence. Secondly, one can examine individual factors, levels or combinations of factors and/or levels for similarities or differences. Finally, if the investigation has taken place in the region of an 'optimum' condition and one has an appropriate number of levels, one can optimize the system. Optimization gives one a solution to a problem which maximizes or minimizes a response in the region of lowest possible variability.

Distributions

Three other tests often used in handling data are the "t" distribution, the "F" test, and the Analysis of Variance (ANOVA).

The "t" distribution test is used to determine the significance of difference between measures of central tendencies of two samples and when samples are small and sigma is unknown. The "t" distribution resembles the normal curve, except that is flatter and broader, reflecting the greater variability of small samples. The "t" distribution tables are utilized to determine critical values for comparison to the calculated "t" statistic. The "t" test can be used for one or two tailed tests and it can be conducted based on two small samples. Each sample is averaged and the differences are divided by the pooled standard deviation. This statistic is then compared to the critical value statistic found in the "t" tables.

The "F" test is used to compare two population variances, that is, the precision of multiple manufacturing/measuring devices or the significance of differences among the spread of samples. Intuitively one compares 2 population variances using ratios. When the ratio is equal to one, there is little evidence to indicate populations are unequal. A very large or small difference in the ratio would provide evidence that the populations are different. The questions then becomes, when do we reject the null hypothesis: To answer this we must first take repeated samples and study the distribution. The "F" test is used by finding the degrees of freedom in the denominator and the numerator and finding their intersection point from the F Table. For example F is calculated by dividing the variability of one sample into the variability of the other and squaring the result, that is,

$$F = \left(\frac{\text{variability of 1 lot X n/n-1}}{\text{variability of 2nd lot X n/n-1}} \right)^2$$

If the value is determined to be insignificant or less than the values in the F Tables, the variances may be considered equal.

Analysis of Variance (ANOVA)

This experimental design permits the randomization of all factors. When a process has two or more factors affecting the variability, the interpretation of the relative contribution of each of these factors to the total variability can be made using a statistical total variance of the process is equal to the sum of the components' variance if the factors are acting independently. The advantage of the method is that where several factors are involved in a process or in the quality of the product, it is possible to rank their effects on the total variation in order of magnitude. Thus, the information is useful in the determination as to where to place efforts to reduce variability for maximum improvement with a minimum expenditure of time and effort. The interpretation of the statistic is significant if it is equal to or greater than the value from the F table at the level of significance selected. If the statistic is significant, the least significance difference (LSD) is calculated to determine where the difference among the varients lie. The LSD is the minimum by which the means of any two rows or columns significantly differ from each other. If the statistic is not significant at the chosen level, the LSD is not calculated.

The researcher should obtain STAT View and GRAPHICS software or similar programs for use with personal computers (PC's) or more complicated systems using Main Frame Computers. The researcher must learn to gather data and learn to analyze data for continuous improvements within a given food firm to stay competitive. Of course, nature has many posibilities that await our discovery. Even the best designed experiments and the most sophisticated software may never reveal all her secrets. However, data gathering and the interpretation of the facts are major responsibilities of the food researcher today to keep his or her firm competitive.

FIGURE 14.1 — Testing The Significance Between Two Sample Means

N_1	X_1	Method I $X_1{}^2$	N_2	X_2	Method II $X_2{}^2$
1	0.020	0.000400	1	0.010	0.000100
2	0.020	0.000400	2	0.022	0.000484
3	0.015	0.000225	3	0.029	0.000841
4	0.003	0.000009	4	0.009	0.000081
5	0.015	0.000225	5	0.036	0.001296
6	0.014	0.000196	6	0.023	0.000529
7	0.010	0.000100	7	0.010	0.000100
8	0.028	0.000784	8	0.025	0.000625
9	0.020	0.000400	9	0.021	0.000441
10	0.008	0.000064	10	0.034	0.001156
11	0.010	0.000100	11	0.010	0.000100
12	0.031	0.000961	12	0.010	0.000100

$X_1 = 0.194 \qquad X_1{}^2 = 0.003864 \qquad X_2 = 0.239 \qquad X_2{}^2 = 0.005853$
$\overline{X}_1 = 0.0161 = X_1/N_1 \qquad\qquad\qquad \overline{X}_2 = 0.0199 = X_2/N_2$

Notes:

1. $(\overline{X}_1 - \overline{X}_2)^2 = (0.0161 - 0.0199)^2 = 0.00001444$

2. $\Sigma X'_1{}^2 = \Sigma X_1{}^2 - (\Sigma X_1)^2/N = 0.003864 - (0.194)^2/12 =$
   $\qquad\qquad\qquad\qquad\qquad 0.003864 - 0.003136 = 0.000728$
   $\Sigma X'_2{}^2 = \Sigma X_2{}^2 - (\Sigma X_2)^2/N = 0.005853 - (0.239)^2/12 =$
   $\qquad\qquad\qquad\qquad\qquad 0.005853 - 0.004760 = 0.001093$

3. $(1/N_1 + 1/N_2) = (1/12 + 1/12) = 0.0833 + 0.0833 = 0.1666$

4. $S'^2 = \dfrac{\Sigma X_1{}^2 + \Sigma X_2{}^2}{N_1 + N_2 - 2} = \dfrac{0.009717}{22} = 0.00044168$

5. $(S'^2)(1/N_1 + 1/N_2) = (0.00044168)(0.1666) = 0.0000735839$

6. $F = (\overline{X}_1 - \overline{X}_2)^2 / ((S'^2)(1/N_1 + 1/N_2)) = 0.00001444 / 0.0000735839 = 0.19624$

The F table shows a 5% value of 4.30 for $N_1 + N_2 - 2 = 22$ degrees of freedom which is larger than 0.19624. Therefore, no significant difference between these means has been shown.

FIGURE 14.2 — Statistical Analysis Form

Technologist_____ Date _____

Code_____   Code_____

Sample	X_1	$X_1{}^2$	X_2	$X_2{}^2$

Sums

Average

FIGURE 14.3 — 5% Points For The Distribution of F

f1 degrees of freedom (for greater mean square)

f2	1	2	3	4	5	6	7	8	9	10	100	500
1	161	200	216	225	230	234	237	239	241	242	253	254
2	18.51	19.00	19.16	19.25	19.30	19.33	19.36	19.37	19.38	19.39	19.49	19.50
3	10.13	9.55	9.28	9.12	9.01	8.94	8.88	8.84	8.81	8.78	8.56	8.54
4	7.71	6.94	6.59	6.39	6.26	6.16	6.09	6.04	6.00	5.96	5.66	5.64
5	6.61	5.79	5.41	5.19	5.05	4.95	4.88	4.82	4.78	4.74	4.40	4.37
6	5.99	5.14	4.76	4.53	4.39	4.28	4.21	4.15	4.10	4.06	3.71	3.68
7	5.59	4.74	4.35	4.12	3.97	3.87	3.79	3.73	3.68	3.63	3.28	3.24
8	5.32	4.46	4.07	3.84	3.69	3.58	3.50	3.44	3.39	3.34	2.98	2.94
9	5.12	4.26	3.86	3.63	3.48	3.37	3.29	3.23	3.18	3.13	2.76	2.72
10	4.96	4.10	3.71	3.48	3.33	3.22	3.14	3.07	3.02	2.97	2.59	2.55
11	4.84	3.98	3.59	3.36	3.20	3.09	3.01	2.95	2.90	2.86	2.45	2.41
12	4.75	3.88	3.49	3.26	3.11	3.00	2.92	2.85	2.80	2.76	2.35	2.31
13	4.67	3.80	3.41	3.18	3.02	2.92	2.84	2.77	2.72	2.67	2.26	2.22
14	4.60	3.74	3.34	3.11	2.96	2.85	2.77	2.70	2.65	2.60	2.19	2.14
15	4.54	3.68	3.29	3.06	2.90	2.79	2.70	2.64	2.59	2.55	2.12	2.08
16	4.49	3.63	3.24	3.01	2.85	2.74	2.66	2.59	2.54	2.49	2.07	2.02
17	4.45	3.59	3.20	2.96	2.81	2.70	2.62	2.55	2.50	2.45	2.02	1.97
18	4.41	3.55	3.16	2.93	2.77	2.66	2.58	2.51	2.46	2.41	1.98	1.93
19	4.38	3.52	3.13	2.90	2.74	2.63	2.55	2.48	2.43	2.38	1.94	1.90
20	4.35	3.49	3.10	2.87	2.71	2.60	2.52	2.45	2.40	2.35	1.90	1.85
21	4.32	3.47	3.07	2.84	2.68	2.57	2.49	2.42	2.37	2.32	1.87	1.82
22	4.30	3.44	3.05	2.82	2.66	2.55	2.47	2.40	2.35	2.30	1.84	1.80
23	4.28	3.42	3.03	2.80	2.64	2.53	2.45	2.38	2.32	2.28	1.82	1.77
24	4.26	3.40	3.01	2.78	2.62	2.51	2.43	2.36	2.30	2.26	1.80	1.74
25	4.24	3.38	2.99	2.76	2.60	2.49	2.41	2.34	2.28	2.24	1.77	1.72
30	4.17	3.32	2.92	2.69	2.53	2.42	2.34	2.27	2.21	2.16	1.69	1.64
50	4.03	3.18	2.79	2.56	2.40	2.29	2.20	2.13	2.07	2.02	1.52	1.46
100	3.94	3.09	2.70	2.46	2.30	2.19	2.10	2.03	1.97	1.92	1.39	1.30
200	3.89	3.04	2.65	2.41	2.26	2.14	2.05	1.98	1.92	1.87	1.32	1.22

FIGURE 14.4 — 5% Points For The Distribution of F

f1 degrees of freedom (for greater mean square)

f2	1	2	3	4	5	6	7	8	9	10	100	500
1	4,052	4,999	5,403	5,625	5,764	5,859	5,928	5,981	6,022	6,056	6,334	6,361
2	98.49	99.00	99.17	99.25	99.30	99.33	99.34	99.36	99.38	99.40	99.49	99.50
3	34.12	30.82	29.46	28.71	28.24	27.91	27.67	27.49	27.34	27.23	26.23	26.14
4	21.20	18.00	16.69	15.98	15.52	15.21	14.98	14.80	14.66	14.54	13.57	13.48
5	16.26	13.27	12.06	11.39	10.97	10.67	10.45	10.27	10.15	10.05	9.13	9.04
6	13.74	10.92	9.78	9.15	8.75	8.47	8.26	8.10	7.98	7.87	6.99	6.90
7	12.25	9.55	8.45	7.85	7.46	7.19	7.00	6.84	6.71	6.62	5.75	5.67
8	11.26	8.65	7.59	7.01	6.63	6.37	6.19	6.03	5.91	5.82	4.96	4.88
9	10.56	8.02	6.99	6.42	6.06	5.80	5.62	5.47	5.35	5.26	4.41	4.33
10	10.04	7.56	6.55	5.99	5.64	5.39	5.21	5.06	4.95	4.85	4.01	3.93
11	9.65	7.20	6.22	5.67	5.32	5.07	4.88	4.74	4.63	4.54	3.70	3.62
12	9.33	6.93	5.95	5.41	5.06	4.82	4.65	4.50	4.39	4.30	3.46	3.38
13	9.07	6.70	5.74	5.20	4.86	4.62	4.44	4.30	4.19	4.10	3.27	3.18
14	8.86	6.51	5.56	5.03	4.69	4.46	4.28	4.14	4.03	3.94	3.11	3.02
15	8.68	6.36	5.42	4.89	4.56	4.32	4.14	4.00	3.89	3.80	2.97	2.89
16	8.53	6.23	5.29	4.77	4.44	4.20	4.03	3.89	3.78	3.69	2.86	2.77
17	8.40	6.11	5.18	4.67	4.34	4.10	3.93	3.79	3.68	3.59	2.76	2.67
18	8.28	6.01	5.09	4.58	4.25	4.01	3.85	3.71	3.60	3.51	2.68	2.59
19	8.18	5.93	5.01	4.50	4.17	3.94	3.77	3.63	3.52	3.43	2.60	2.51
20	8.10	5.85	4.94	4.43	4.10	3.87	3.71	3.56	3.45	3.37	2.53	2.44
21	8.02	5.78	4.87	4.37	4.04	3.81	3.65	3.51	3.40	3.31	2.47	2.38
22	7.94	5.72	4.82	4.31	3.99	3.76	3.59	3.45	3.35	3.26	3.42	2.33
23	7.88	5.66	4.76	4.26	3.94	3.71	3.54	3.41	3.30	3.21	2.37	2.28
24	7.82	5.61	4.72	4.22	3.90	3.67	3.50	3.36	3.25	3.17	2.33	2.23
25	7.77	5.57	4.68	4.18	3.86	3.63	3.46	3.32	3.21	3.13	2.29	2.19
30	7.56	5.39	4.51	4.02	3.70	3.47	3.30	3.17	3.06	2.98	2.13	2.03
50	7.17	5.06	4.20	3.72	3.41	3.18	3.02	2.88	2.78	2.70	1.82	1.71
100	6.90	4.82	3.98	3.51	3.20	2.99	2.82	2.69	2.59	2.51	1.59	1.46
200	6.76	4.71	3.88	3.41	3.11	2.90	2.73	2.60	2.50	2.41	1.48	1.33

FIGURE 14.5 — Two-Way Analysis of Variance for Yield of 5 Cultivars over A 4 Year Period

| | Year | | | | | |
Cultivar	1	2	3	4	Sum	Average
GP 467	26	20	30	77	153	38.2
Early Gallaten	32	41	25	92	190	47.5
GP 68-115	50	55	45	59	209	52.2
GP 317	10	30	30	45	115	28.8
Wondergreen	35	40	36	85	196	49.0
Sum	153	186	166	358	863	
Average	30.6	37.2	33.2	71.6		

A. $863^2/ 20 = 37238.45$
B. $46001 - 37238.45 = 8762.55$
C. $213725/5 - 37238.45 = 5506.55$
D. $154831.00/4 - 37238.45 = 1469.30$
E. 1786.70
See SQC Form 6.5 for equations.

Source	Sum of Squares	Degrees of Freedom	Mean Square	F
Year	5506.55	3	1835.52	12.33
Cultivar	1469.30	4	367.33	2.47
Error	1786.70	12	148.89	
Total	8762.55			

Book F values = 3.49 at 5% level of significance
5.95 at 1% level of significance

LSD for Year:
= $\sqrt{\ ^{2}/_{5} \times 148.89 \times 5.95}$ = 18.82

Interpretation

Year	Average Yield
1	30.6
2	37.2
3	33.2
4	71.6

Thus the fourth year had a significantly higher yield than years 1, 2 and 3. There were no significant differences in the yield among the cultivars.

FIGURE 14.6 — Two-Way Analysis of Variance

Summary of Data:

Row	A	B	C	D	E	etc.	Sum	Mean
			Column					
1							Sums	
2							of	
3							Rows	
etc.								
Sum			Sums of Columns				Grand Sum	

Analysis of Data

Source of Variance	Sum of Squares	Degrees of Freedom	Mean Square	F
Variate i-columns	C	(No. of Columns − 1)	$x = \dfrac{(C)}{\text{No. of Col.} - 1}$	x/z
Variate j-rows	D	(No. of Rows − 1)	$y = \dfrac{(D)}{\text{No. of Rows} - 1}$	or y/z
Error	E	(No. Col. − 1) (No. Rows− 1)	$\dfrac{(E)}{(\text{Col.} - 1)(\text{Rows} - 1)} = z$	
Total	B			

A. (Grand Sum)^2 / total number of observations = c
B. (Square all observations and add) − c
C. [(Sum of observations in one column squared and add to same for other columns) / (no. of rows)] − c
D. [(Sum of observations in one row squared and add to same for rows) / (no. of columns)] − c
E. (B) − [(C) + (D)]

CHAPTER 15

Samples and Sampling

Many people doing quality assurance work and, yes even research studies, rely on "grab samples" rather than using a statistical sampling plan for obtaining samples to assure quality.

A sample to be valid for product or process control and evaluation must be representative of the lot or run and it must be selected randomly. Modern acceptance sampling procedures are usually used to make decisions whether to accept and/or reject lots of product produced as opposed to control charts used during manufacture to assure that the product is in conformity to the specifications. Even with control charting, sampling is a prerequisite to charting the data. By far, the sample is the greatest limiting factor in the successful control of product quality.

The United States Department of Agriculture has adopted a statistical plan and regulations governing inspection and certification of processed fruits and vegetables and related food products. The specific procedures, including tables for sample plans, definitions, statistical quality control and acceptance levels are found in Title 7 (Part 52) of the Code of Federal Regulations. Figures 15.1, 15.2, 15.3, and 15.4 are the USDA Sampling Plan for Canned Fruits and Vegetables, Frozen Products, Dried or Low Moisture Products, and Liquid and Homogeneous Products.

As noted in Figure 15.1, the user must first:
  (1) identify the size of container for any given product under a given code, and
  (2) know the actual lot size.

A lot is defined as any number of containers of the same size, type and style located in the same plant, warehouse, commerical storage, railway car, truck, or any other conveyance or storage facility:— Provided, that the number of containers comprising a lot may not exceed the maximum number specified for a sample size of 60.— Normally for quality assurance personnel, no lot should exceed a shift and preferably this lot should not exceed more than 4 hours of operations.

In using information in Figure 15.1, the QA person after determining the lot size and container size reads the sample size and acceptance number directly from the bottom of the table. For example, lets suppose we have a lot of 100,000 containers of No. 303 size cans. The sample size would be 29 containers and we would accept the lot if no more than 4 deviated from the standard or specifications upon inspection.

If we were making an on-line inspection our sample size would only be 21 containers and our accpetance number would be 3. As one can see this is a rather simple method of determining the number of samples to select. However, obtaining representative samples is another matter, whether from the warehouse, truck, or on-line.

The Regulations governing the sampling procedures for determination of nutrient composition of foods are published in Title 21, Para 1.17 Food: Nutritional Labeling and it states that a collection of primary containers or units of the same size, type, and style produced under conditions as nearly uniform as posible, designated by a common container code or marking, or the absence of any common container code or marking a day's production constitutes a lot. The sample for nutrient analysis shall consist of a composite of 12 sub-samples (consumer units) taken one from each of 12 different randomly chosen shipping cases to be representative of a lot.

U.S. Patent Number 4.580,226 granted in 1986 to Roger Bennison was for a system of random sampling. His patent describes an apparatus and process for randomly selecting samples for removal from production lines. The operator chooses the total number of samples from which the random selection is to be made. A series of random numbers, each representing an incremental advancement of the production is developed when a reset bottom is actuated by the operator on a micro-computer, thereby establishing a starting point. A sensor senses the articles as they pass a predetermined station, and those articles are removed from the advancing series. This apparatus should be of value to the food industry to aid in the assurance of proper selection of random samples to assure quality during given production runs.

Probably the most valuable aid in selecting any sampling plan is the Operational Characteristic Curve (OCC). This permits one to evaluate the operation of the sampling plan under varying conditions of incoming materials and of the products produced. It is an excellent method of illustrating the risks inherent in all sampling plans. The Operating Curve (OC) depends upon two parameters, that is the sample size "N" and the acceptance number "c". The acceptable quality level (AQL) is the level of quality that you want the plan to accept a "high" percentage of the time. This is usually set by company policy to balance the cost of:

1. Finding and correcting a defect,
2. Loss incurred if a defective unit gets out, and,
3. The purchasing agreement.

To make an OC curve or sampling plan more to your liking, the acceptance number "c" can be increased by shifting to the right to help the producer get greater acceptance of the lot. On the other hand, if the consumer wants a tighter plan, the acceptance number can be increased and shifted to the left. If one wants to change both as far as risks are concerned, increase "N" with "c" increased proportionately. The curve becomes steeper and the plan becomes more discriminating.

The index (AQL) used to define quality should reflect the needs of the consumer and the producer and not be chosen primarily for statistical convenience. The sampling risks should be known in quantitative forms (OC curve). The producer should have adequate protection against any rejection of good lots and the consumer should be protected against acceptance of bad lots. The plan should minimize the total cost of inspection of all products. This requires careful evaluation of the pros and cons of attributes and variable plans, and single, double, and multiple sampling plans. The plan should build in flexibility to reflect changes in lot sizes, quality of product submitted, and other pertinent facts.

The advantages of sampling plans include the following:
1. Saving in cost to the firm, and
2. Economy of sampling a few versus 100% inspection.

Sampling plans are a must if one is doing destructive testing. Sampling plans permit less time to perform the evaluation, less handling of products, fewer inspectors are required, and improved level of quality acceptance, and most importantly, improved vendor and vendee relationships. However, there are Alpha (Producers risks, that is, rejecting when you should be accepting) and Beta (Consumer risks, that is, accepting when you should be rejecting) risks involved, it takes time to document the prescribed procedures and there is less information when compared to 100% inspection. In using sampling plans one must eliminate bias in measurements and judgement.

Thus, it should be obvious that there are better methods of sampling than the "grab sample" method. The best way is none too good to insure the quality of any run or lot because of the wide variation that constantly exists in any given food operations.

Quality assurance personnel including the operator who has control of a given unit operation or the process must utilize appropriate sampling practices and procedures to assure product quality and/or process control.

Process control will distinguish between special causes and common causes of variation and aid management in producing products according to the customers' expectations. When a process is said to be in control, the source of variation is from common causes and these are up to management to:

(1)-eliminate for the production of more uniform products,
(2)-improvement of their competitive position within the industry,
(3)-increase employee moral in the workplace,
(4)-lower costs of production,
(5)-provide greater profits,
(6)-assure their future position in the industry, and
(7)-provide the customer with what they expect all the time.

FIGURE 15.1 — Canned or Similarly Processed Fruits, Vegetables, and Products
Containing Units of Such Size and Character as to be readily separable
Sampling Plans and Acceptance Levels

Container Size Group	Lot Size (Number of Containers)[1]							
Group 1: Any type container of a volume not exceeding that of a No. 303 size can.	3,000 or less	3,001 – 12,000	12,001 – 39,000	39,001 – 84,000	84,001 – 145,000	145,001 – 228,000	228,001 – 336,000	336,001 – 480,000
Group 2: Any type of container of a volume exceeding that of a No. 303 size can but not exceeding that of a No. 3 cyclinder size can.	1,500 or less	1,501 – 6,000	6,001 – 19,500	19,501 – 42,000	42,001 – 72,500	72,501 – 114,000	114,001 – 168,000	168,001 – 240,000
Group 3: Any type of container of a volume exceeding that of a No. 3 cylinder size can, but not exceeding that of a No. 12 size can.	750 or less	751 – 3,000	3,001 – 9,750	9,751 – 21,000	21,001 – 36,250	36,251 – 57,000	57,001 – 84,000	84,001 – 120,000
Group 4: Any type of container of a volume exceeding that of a No. 12 size can.	Convert to equivalent number of 6-pound net weight containers and use group 3							
Lot inspection:								
Sample size (number of sample units)[2]	3	6	13	21	29	38	48	60
Acceptance number	0	1	2	3	4	5	6	7
On-line in-plant inspection:								
Sample size (number of sample units)[2]	3	6	6	13	21	29	38	48
Acceptance number	0	1	1	2	3	4	5	6

[1] Under on-line in-plant inspection, a 5 percent overrun in number of containers may be permitted by the inspector before going to the next larger sample size.

[2] When a standard sample unit size is not specified in the U.S. grade standards, the sample units for the various container size groups are as follows: Groups 1, 2, and 3—1 container and its entire contents. Group 4 approximately 2 pounds of product. When determined by the inspector that a 2-pound sample unit is inadequate, a larger sample unit may be substituted.

FIGURE 15.2 — Frozen or Similarly Processed Fruits, Vegetables and Products Containing Units of Such Size and Character as to be readily separable

Container Size Group	Lot Size (Number of Containers)[1]							
Group 1: Any type of container of 1 pound or less net weight	2,400 or less	2,401– 9,600	9,601– 31,200	31,201– 67,200	67,201– 116,000	116,001– 182,400	182,401– 268,800	268,801– 384,000
Group 2: Any type of container over 1 pound but not over 2½ pounds net weight	1,200 or less	1,201– 4,800	4,801– 15,600	15,601– 33,600	33,601– 58,000	58,001– 91,200	91,201– 134,400	134,401– 192,000
Group 3: Any type of container over 2½ pounds	Convert to equivalent number of 2½-pound containers and use group 2							
Lot Inspection								
Sample size (number of sample units)[2]	3	6	13	21	29	38	48	60
Acceptance number	0	1	2	3	4	5	6	7
On-line in-plant inspection:								
Sample size (number of sample units)[2]	3	6	6	13	21	29	38	48
Acceptance number	0	1	1	2	3	4	5	6

[1]Under on-line in-plant inspection, a 5% overrun in number of containers may be permitted by the inspector before going to the next larger sample size.

[2]When a standard sample unit size is not specified in the U.S. standards, the sample units for the various groups are as follows: Groups 1 and 2—1 container and its entire contents. Group 3 containers up to 10 pounds—approximately 3 pounds of product. When determined by the inspector that a 3-pound sample unit is inadequate, a larger sample unit of 1 or more containers and their entire contents may be substituted for 1 or more sample units of 3 pounds.

FIGURE 15.3 — Canned, Frozen, or otherwise Processed Fruits, Vegetables, Related Products of a Comminuted Fluid or Homogeneous State

Container Size Group	Lot Size (Number of Containers)[1]							
Group 1: Any type of container of 1 pound or less	4,500 or less	4,501– 18,000	18,001– 58,000	58,501– 126,000	126,001– 217,000	217,001– 342,000	342,001– 504,000	504,001– 720,000
Group 2: Any type of container exceeding 1 pound but not exceeding 60 ounces	3,000 or less	3,001– 12,000	12,001– 39,000	39,001– 84,000	84,000– 145,000	145,001– 223,000	228,001– 336,000	336,001– 480,000
Group 3: Any type of container exceeding 60 ounces but not exceeding 10 pounds	1,500 or less	1,501– 6,000	6,001– 19,500	19,501– 42,000	42,001– 72,500	72,501– 114,000	114,001– 168,000	168,001– 240,00
Group 4: Any type of container exceeding 10 pounds	Convert to equivalent number of 6-pound containers and use group 3							
Lot inspection: Sample size (number of sample units)[2]	3	6	13	21	29	38	48	60
Acceptance number	0	1	2	3	4	5	6	7
On-line in-plant inspection Sample size (number of sample units)[2]	3	6	6	13	21	29	38	48
Acceptance number	0	1	1	2	3	4	5	6

[1]Under on-line in-plant inspection, a 5% overrun in number of containers may be permitted by the inspector before going to the next larger sample size.

[2]When a standard sample unit size is not specified in the U.S. grade standards, the sample units for the various container size groups are as follows: Groups 1, 2, and 3—1 container and its entire contents. A smaller sample unit may be substituted in group 3 at the inspectors' discretion. Group 4—approximately 16 ounces of product. When determined by the inspector that a 16-ounce sample unit is inadequate, a larger sample unit may be substituted.

FIGURE 15.4 — Dehydrated (Low Moisture) Fruits and Vegetables

Container Size Group	Lot Size (Number of Containers)[1]							
Group 1: Any type of container of 1 pound or less, net weight	1,800 or less	1,801– 7,200	7,201– 23,400	23,401– 54,000	50,401– 87,000	87,001– 136,000	136,801– 201,000	201,601– 288,000
Group 2: Any type of container over 1 pound but not over 6 pounds net weight	600 or less	601– 2,400	2,401– 7,800	7,801– 16,800	16,801– 29,000	29,001– 45,600	45,601– 67,200	67,201– 96,000
Group 3: Any type of container over 6 pounds	Convert to equivalent number of 5-pound containers and use group 2							
Lot inspection:								
Sample size (No. of sample units)[2]	3	6	13	21	29	38	48	60
Acceptance number	0	1	2	3	4	5	6	7
One-line in-plant inspection Sample size (No. of sample units)[2]	3	6	6	13	21	29	38	48

[1] Under on-line in-plant inspection, a 5% overrun in number of containers may be permitted by the inspector before going to the next larger sample size.

[2] When a standard sample unit size is not specified in the U.S. standards, the sample units for the various groups are as follows: Groups 1 and 2—1 container and its entire contents. Group 3 containers up to 10 pounds—approximately 3 pounds of product. When determined by the inspector that a 3-pound sample unit is inadequate, a larger sample unit of 1 or more containers and their entire contents may be substituted for 1 or more sample units of 3 pounds.

FIGURE 15.5 — An Operating Characteristic Curve

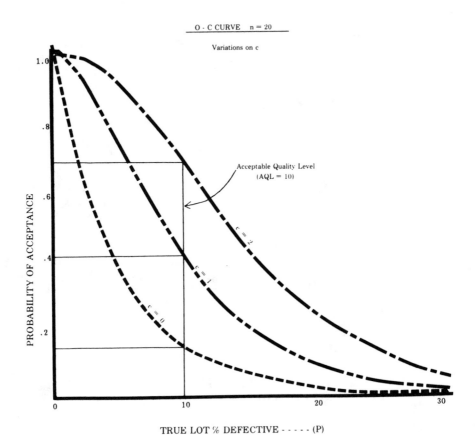

CHAPTER 16

Communications

Communication should be of prime importance in the success of Total Quality Management. It all starts with the President, CEO, and Top Management setting the stage by publishing their Policy Statement, their Mission document, and their Goals and Objectives for the firm. These documents need to be part of the everyday standard operating procedures for the firm. Ideally, they should be announced in the firm's house organ or other usual channels of communication within the firm. The documents should be consistent in terminology, they should be clear in their statements, and they should always be most optimistic.

Of course, at the same time the above is happening, the firm should have in place a "change agent" or some one designated to lead the firm into the change over and through Total Quality Management. This person must help people to realize that changes are going to be made to keep the company competitive and a leader within the industry. This person must have great stature and credibility to overcome the natural resistance to change within the firm. His or her task is a major challenge, but one that must be pursued if the goals and objectives are to be reached. Leadership ability, perseverance, and understanding the basics of human relations are keys for success.

Hopefully, all in management have been trained in TQM and the art of communicating and that they are all 100% behind the need for the change over. Further, if the firm is unionized, the steward should be thoroughly familiar with TQM and he or she fully endorses the plan.

CommFunciation is defined as the process of sending and receiving of messages. The sender stimulates meaning in the mind of the receiver by means of a message conveyed using symbols, noise, motion, etc. The receiver responds by feedback with noise, symbols, motion, etc. The communication should not be complete until the sender is sure the receiver has completely understood the message and responded accordingly.

Communications must be a two-way street. Communications means demonstrating patience, being an active listener, awareness, and searching for meaning. Communications is the exchange of thoughts, opinions, or information by speaking, writing, or signs. Most importantly communications means to transmit knowledge, thoughts, hopes, qualities, or properties.

Of course, in addition to verbal communication, much of communication is via pictures or the written word. Many people in food plants may not understand the spoken word, but they can see pictures and most can read. Pictures with diagrams, charts, etc. are a great way to communicate especially when they are put in video.

Hopman states that we were born to communicate, but our ability to effectively communicate is learned. Communication must be managed and continuously improved.

There may be some barriers to communication, such as,

1. Lack of awareness of any need or any problems,
2. No acceptance of ownership of the problems,
3. Lack of commitment on the part of the individual to solve problems,
4. Inadequate training or understanding of the problem,
5. Lack of cooperation and high degree of animosity between people, between shifts, etc., and
6. Poor communicating skills - people do not like to read, write, and/or listen.

Effective communication systems include the following:

1. Tools or methods that all can understand

2. Involvement of all concerned in the development of the methods of communication,

3. Elimination of fear of involvement, and

4. Proper training of people to communicate (read, write, listen, speak, body motion, and feedback).

Communication means asking the right questions, listening for answers and ideas, and focusing in on what is being said. All questions must be open ended questions. Communications means awareness, demonstrating patience, searching for meanings, and exchanging thoughts and opinions by speaking, writing, sign language including body actions. To communicate one must transmit knowledge, thoughts, hope, qualities, and properties.

Quimby, et al, suggests a need to focus direct attention to provide the greatest payoff for communicating efforts as follows:

1. Leadership based on a true understanding of how quality will influence the success of the organization. Such things as the assessment of the business, what quality improvement will do for job security, and how the firm plans to meet the competition head on.

2. Alignment of business needs, quality plans, and individual actions.

3. The setting for quality priorities and projects that will impact on the business with expected payback. Such things as (a) agreement on business problems including forecasting sales, (b) assignment of responsibilities for placing and implementing quality projects, (c) establishment of problem identification and team assignment.

4. Continuous training programs with workshops and seminars to constantly keep personnel updated.

Employees need to be brought into the fold in small groups of teams. These small groups or teams need to become the leaders of the movement. They need to fully understand the reason for the change over and they need to endorse with their thoughts, their expressions, their concerns and their opinions. The first and most important rule of TQM is that you cannot improve what is not understood. Everyone must have the right information at the right place and at the right time. Further, management must understand rule No. 2 and, that is, communication is a two way street. Feedback is a great part of the process of communication as well as management being a good listener.

Most importantly, communication is sincerely appreciated when a firm learns to celebrate after progress moves forward in the change over program of TQM. The firm should find the time to pause, rejoice, and recognize all those that have made each achievement possible.

CHAPTER 17

The Cost of Quality

Quality costs are defined as the costs which exist in the design, development, manufacture, and distribution of a product, a process, or a service because a quality deficiency either does or might exist. These costs would disappear if all possible quality defficiencies disappeared and if the firm had perfect control of materials (ingredients, products, packaging materials, utilities, etc.), people, and processes.

The cost of quality is the cost of doing things wrong. Crosby calls it the Price of Non-Conformance (PONC). It is the cost of doing things over; throwing the finished product out or away because of not meeting specifications; and pulling the product from the market because of poor quality, that is, recalls. Probably more important than any of these three items is the reaction by the buyer to products that do not meet their expectations. Once the customer purchases a bad product, they may not return and they tell many other customers of their plight. The reaction becomes a "snow-ball" effect. The food industry cannot afford unhappy customers. One author refers to this as the "market damage" cost.

Crosby figures that if an organization concentrates on improving quality, it can probably increase its profits by 5 to 10 percent of its sales. Other authors indicate that from 15 percent to 40 percent of the plants productivity is spent on correcting mistakes.

Henry and Knowler state that there are two broad categories of
quality costs (I have added areas where appropriate and in italics):

I Direct costs or costs of good quality
  A. Prevention Costs
    1. Design reviews
    2. Pre-production runs (debugging)
    3. Set-up adjustments
    4. Process control
    5. Purchasing quality control (vendor survey)
    6. Preventive maintenance
    7. *Cost of training*

  B. Appraisal Costs
    1. Estimation of Quality levels
    2. Audits of the system (*SPC charts, package integrity checks,
    acceptable quality levels on incoming materials (AQL's)*)

II Indirect Costs or costs of poor quality
  A. Internal failures
    1 Scrap
    2. Rework
    3. Material review board activity-(embargoes products)
    4. *Costs to reprocess and/or recoup*
  B. External Failures
    1. Customer complaints
    2. Excess shipping charges
    3. Loss of customers
    4. Product liability suits
    5. Paper work

To achieve a favorable return on the investment (ROI) of materials,
processes, and people the above four categories of quality costs must be
determined to establish a benchmark for comparison. Most companies
will find that there is considerable inbalance between the dollars spent
in the value added area of prevention and appraisal. This type of dollar
breakdown will focus where improvement projects can and should be
undertaken.

Total quality costs alone do not provide a clear picture to management. They should be compared to various parts of the business that identify change, that is, a labor base, production costs, sales or per unit produced in order to aid in providing a realistic review of present performance and to assist in appraising future potentials.

Through the use of computers and "spread sheet" programs, firms should be able to quickly get a handle on their quality costs. Input from various facets of the operation should identify problem areas so that appropriate adjustments can be made to clarify the problems. Once data is generated, that is, "where are we" the use of charts and graphs will help to shed light on the opportunity areas to correct quality costs problems.

By clearly identifying and communicating the financial impact of the cost of quality, management can establish appropriate objectives and a strategy to achieve consumer enthusiasm and their expectations all the time.

CHAPTER 18

Rewards & Recognitions

To me, being recognized for an honest effort is the most humbling experience I know of. I happen to think that people like to be recognized and people like to be rewarded for a job well done. It is a tremendous way to boost one's moral and to show appreciation for a job well done.

Rewards may come in many forms, some are as follows:

(1) Calling a person by their first name;

(2) Providing bonus (s) for making significant contributions;

(3) Earning merit (s) which can be redeemed for gifts or prizes;

(4) Seeing one's picture with a story or write-up in the "house organ", local papers, and/or in appropriate trade journals;

(5) Public praise in front of peers, supervisors, management, etc;

(6) Being invited to a celebration, that is, a breakfast, luncheon, dinners, parties, etc.; and

(7) An opportunity to meet the CEO, Board of Directors, Outstanding Leaders in Government, etc.

In other words recognition and rewards come in many forms and they should aways be positive. This is what most people really want.

The giving of something to take home and share with family and friends is most appropriate, that is, plaques, (metal with appropriate engraving or otherwise), trophies, symbols (the banana award), watches or clocks, etc. These are all most significant to the awardee and they leave a most lasting impression. (I still value my first award, a small engraved plaque, as the Commissioner for Little League Baseball, some 45 years ago).

Another way to recognize people is to present them with an award for years of service. These can start after X years, that is, 10 or even 25 years, and be presented every five years. Many department stores recognize people for longevity. Longevity awards are excellent. But, I really believe this type of recognition needs to be tied to actual contribution to the growth and success of the firm. Too many times, longevity awards alone leads to complacency that may mean less productivity because of the recognition.

Weekly or monthly awards might include weekly parking privileges, saving bonds, trip to vacation spot, etc. The idea is that these are considered incentives for effective achievements and the firm wishes to recognize individuals for their efforts.

By far the greatest award or form of recognition in my opinion is to recognize people by giving them new responsibilities. People like to feel important and adding to their list of responsibilities is a significant way of recognizing them. Of course, they must be held accountable and they must fulfil their responsibilities.

Some managers or supervisors have the old philosophy that recognizing and rewarding people is not needed because they know when they are doing a good job as they are not being criticized. That is old fashion and it leads to poor morale and should be eliminated. Further, it becomes increasingly difficult with this philosophy to motivate people.

Most importantly, most employees do not like to be bought for their loyalty and commitment. Generally, these approaches of paying for loyalty and commitment back fire in the long run because the "award winners" get in the habit of expecting money. Further, the money is gone very quickly and soon forgotten. In the long run many money " winners" relax after winning and in their mind they feel that they do not justify a money award.

The first requirement ought to be for employees to understand the old rule, that is, I will give an honest day's work for an honest day's pay.

Employees should not have to worry about job security and any incentive that induces this fear or need for a dollar incentive is not in the best interest of good labor/management relations.

A second mistake some firms make is to give employees more money in lieu of giving them recognition, praise and/or making them feel that they belonged to the company. Everyone likes to belong or feel that they have a stake in the operation. Money does not buy loyalty. Recognition does imbue loyalty.

Persico states that a third problem with many reward or recognition systems in organizations is that they fail to acknowledge normal process variance. Employees are often rewarded for performance or results over which they have little or no control. Deming says that such systems are lotteries. Employees see little or no connection between their actual work effort and the results. Failing to establish this connection reduces many rewards to inhouse jokes. In one company, employees joked about whose turn it was to be employee of the month.

Also, it is most important to reward efforts as well as results. This is particularly true when working with teams or groups of people working on process improvement projects. These people are laying the ground work for future successes in the firm. Teams are a most effective way to bring out the strength and enthusiasm of the team members. These teams can have an effective role to play in the future management of many firms. They are putting together building blocks for greater uniformity in quality and more productivity from given processes. Team effort is a significant step in building future relationships with employees and leading the way to the growth and solid foundation of the firm.

Reward and recognitions are positive steps in a firm's growth and stability. If nothing more, it establishes management's interest in their people, the individual employee, and the building of esprit de corps throughout the firm.

CHAPTER 19

Questions to be Answered When Implementing a TQM Program

1. Have we developed a POLICY Statement and communicated this along with our OBJECTIVES and MISSION to all our employees?

2. Are resources properly allocated to support our Total Quality Management Program?

3. Do we have a "Change Agent" or a designated person in house to implement our Total Quality Management program?

4. Have we implemented Total Quality Management (TQM) programs with our suppliers?

5. Are our suppliers showing continuous improvements with their products and services?

6 Are we rating our suppliers on:
   (A) Promptness of Delivery or Just in Time
   (B) Quality, and
   (C) Price ?

7. Do all levels of management give sufficient leadership to mobilize all the skills, knowledge, and positive attitudes among our personnel?

8. Are our employees trained to use statistical process control tools and methods for control of processing, warehousing, marketing, office management, etc.?

9. Are we listening to our employees and their suggestions for quality improvement and productivity problems?

10. Have we adequately trained all our employees in TQM methods and practices?

11. Are we promoting and obtaining team work among our employees?

12. Are we showing significant improvements in the quality of the products we produce?

13. Do we have evidence of productivity improvement?

14. Are we showing improvements in our unit costs of production?

15. Are appropriate management personnel aware of customer complaints?

16. Are customer complaints showing significant reductions?

17. Do we maintain an active program to investigate, initiate corrective action and respond to customer complaints?

18. Are we applying new technologies to improve productivity and quality?

19. Are our values and objectives promoted to all our employees and the public at large?

20. Do we apply new technologies to improve productivity and quality?

21. Do our marketing and sales personnel know and understand the process limitation for all our products?

22. Are our sales personnel alert to customer's needs and expectations and the true state of our competition?

23. Are our cost accountants and purchasing personnel encouraging good quality rather than shoddy performance?

24. Are quality assurance personnel providing adequate training and up-dating of the line personnel?

25. Are our managers "walking the talk" or practicing MBWA, that is managing by walking around?

26. Are we recognizing personnel for their improvements in the reduction of absenteeism?

27. Are we really lowering our inventories and obtaining improvements in our total cycle times of all our products?

28. Do we have a system established and on the calendar for the annual rewards and recognition of our personnel in the TQM program?

29. Have we completed the annual audit of our quality costs?

30. Do we have current data to show the actual dollar cost of the products sold this year versus last year?

31. Do we have current data to show the dollars saved in:
   A - Costs of Ingredients
   B - Costs of Packaging Materials
   C - Inventory of Finished Products

32. Do we have data to show the total system cycle time for the current year versus the past year?

33. Do we have data on the reduction of customer complaints for this year versus the past year?

34. Do we know what our complaints are and have we corrected all known existing problem areas?

35. Do we have data to show improvements this year versus the past year for:

    A. - Reduction in Worker's Compensation Costs

    B. - Lessening of Employee Turnover

    C. - Reduction in Grievance Activity

    D. - Elimination of Alcohol and Drug Abuse among all of our personnel?

36. Are we set up to practice a Continuous Improvement Program for all our employees?

The above are only suggested questions to get started. Each firm should develop their own set of questions to build for the future and search for better relations with their suppliers, their people, their customers, and their public at large.

CHAPTER 20

Launching Your Total Quality Management Program

Getting started is always the hardest part, however, if you have affirmatively answered all the questions in Chapter 19 and you have followed through on the suggestions in the text, it should be easy. Basically, there are just eight steps as follows:

1. Commitment by the President, CEO, and Top Management to "change over". This includes, but not limited to the following:

A. Up-dated Policy Statement,

B. Written and Communicated Goals and Objectives, and

C. Approval of the necessary resources.

All successful quality improvement programs must start from the top, they must set the goal, have the vision, and hopefully, lead the firm to 6 sigma control limits all the time, that is nearly perfect products and services. Further, they must be visible and they must manage by walking around (MBWA), that is, they must walk their talk.

2. Appointment of a "Change Agent" or Director of Total Quality Management with full authority to proceed and change the culture and philosophy of the firm over to operating for greater productivity and improved quality.

3. Determination of where your firm is, that is, take measurements, analyze, and determine the facts to find out if the firm is within acceptable limits. This is sometimes called "benchmarking" or how we are doing compared to the industry. It is using the tools of TQM to bring the firm into line, that is, within acceptable limits of quality control followed by quality improvement and productivity through tracking and charting.

4. Establishment of full in-house training for all employees to better understand variation and the use of the "tools of TQM" with appropriate information for implementing needed changes. Thus, the employee is fully armed to take action when and if needed. This allows employees to make more decisions and feel more intelligent. They are not robots and they do want to be full partners of the operation.

5. Building of teams to work together. This is known as networking to ultimately provide the customer satisfaction through team work. Teams learn to make improvements in quality day by day as they know how to measure and interpret the facts and bring the product into line.

6. Applying the art of communication including holding regular interviews with all personnel to listen and appraise their contributions and the steps that are needed to move the firm ahead to meet and exceed the competition.

7. Focusing on the customer, they are the one the firm must satisfy. Firms grow because they have satisfied customers. The satisfied customer means repeat business and repeat business means more sales.

8. Stopping to pause, at least, once per year to say "thanks" and to recognize and reward:
(1) People and teams for their help in building a better place to work and a better firm for the future,
(2) Suppliers for their promptness of delivery of quality products at the right time and at competitive prices,
(3) Leaders and Supervisors for their vision, their foresight, and their follow through, and their ability to "coach" and lead by example, and
(4) Our Customers for their loyalty and their continued support.

The launching of TQM will be successful by following the above suggestions one step at a time. Some people question the time to fully implement a TQM program and the answer is that it varies based on: (1) the dedication of top management, (2) the "change agent" or Director (3) the interest and enthusiasm of the employees for the change, and, of course, (4), the size of the firm, that is the number of people and number of products being manufactured. In some plants Total Quality

Management can be implemented, at least, in many areas in less than one year while in other plants the time may extend into the third year.

The key is to get started and once started to keep the momentum going. It is a never ending job and improvement in productivity and quality must continue long after the initiation of Total Quality Management. It is all up to the leadership, the change agent, and employees in that order.

The quest for quality is most challenging, it is most rewarding, and it is most fulfilling. People become happy at their work place and their job is most joyful. It is the only way to lead a firm into the next century.

APPENDIX I

Symbols, Abbreviations, Acronyms, and Their Meaning

Symbol	Read	Meanings
a	a	Acceptance No. of defects in a sampling plan
A_2	A sub 2	A factor used to calculate control limits for the average on the X bar chart
Alpha	Alpha	Probability of rejection, sometimes referred to as the producers risk, or risk of the first kind
ANOVA	ANOVA	Analysis of variance
AOQ	AOQ	Average outgoing quality
AOQL	AOQL	Average outgoing quality limit
AQL	AQL	Acceptance quality level-associated with vendor's risk. Minimum number of parts or containers that must comply with quality standards
Ave.	Average	Average, also, indicated by A or X Bar

Symbol	Read	Meaning
Beta	Beta	Probability of acceptance, sometimes called buyer's or consumers risk, or risk of an error of the 2nd kind
c	c	Number of defects or defective units
$\bar{c}$	c Bar	Average number of defects in a sample
CEDAC	CEDAC	Cause and effect diagram and cards which pictorially shows the various causes and how they are related to one another and their effects on a stated cause. Sometimes referred to as the "fishbone chart".
C_p	C sub p	Process capability. This value serves as a guide as to how well the process is in control. It is obtained by dividing the process width (the upper specification-the lower specification width) by the 6 sigma value. Some users calculate the process capability index by 2 times the A value times the R value (see Appendix table of factors for computing control limits) for A sub 2 value if the process is stable.
C_{pk}	C sub pk	This is known as the capability index. The index measures the improvement of the process as firms seek greater uniformity around the desired target. It is calculated by dividing the specification width by the process width. The greater the number the better the index.
CIP	CIP	Continuous improvement process, the goal is zero defects. The Japanese call it Kaizen.
CUSUM	CUSUM	Cumulative sum sampling plan for attributes standards only

Symbol	Read	Meaning
CV	CV	Coefficient of Variability
d_2	d sub 2	A divider of the mean range, R Bar, which will yield an estimate of the standard deviation
D_3	D sub 3	A muliplier of the R Bar to determine the 3 sigma lower control limit on a range chart
D_4	D sub 4	A multiplier of R Bar to determine the 3 sigma upper control limit on a range chart
d.f.	d f	Degrees of freedom
F	F	Frequency
JIT	JIT	Just in time, that is, the elimination of costly inventories.
LSL	LSL	Lower specification limit
LCL	LCL	Lower control limit. This statistic for lower control limit of the average is calculated by multiplying the table value for A sub 2 by the average of the range, R bar and subtracting from the average, that is, $$LCL = X - A_2 \ R$$
LPL	LPL	Lower process limit. This statistic is calculated by subtracting the 3 sigma value from the average of the averages, that is, $$LPL + X - 3_s$$
LSD	LSD	Least significant difference
LRL	LRL	Lower reject limit
LWL	LWL	Lower warning limit

Symbol	Read	Meaning
m	m	Number of subgroups in a sample
Me	Me	Mean
Mi	Mi	Median
Mo	Mo	Mode
n	n	The number of items or observations in a given lot, that is, the number of samples
n_s	n sub s	Number of sample units or measurements for a variable
np	np	An attribute control chart that is used to track the number of individual components that are defective in a given sample.
N	N	Number of items in a given lot to be sampled
OCC	OCC	Operating characteristic curve
$\bar{p}$	p bar	Average percent defective for the process. It is the total number of defects divided by the total number of units inspected and then multiplied by 100, thus, it is expressed in percentages.
POC	POC	Price of conformance
PONC	PONC	Price of non-conformance
QA	QA	Quality assurance, also, Quality audit
QC	QC	Quality control, also, Quality circle
QE	QE	Quality evaluation

Symbol	Read	Meaning
QFD	QFD	Quality function deployment, that is, paying special attention to the customers wants.
QWL	QWL	Quality of work life
r	r	Symbol for the correlation coefficient
R	R	Range, the difference between the largest value and the smallest value in a given set of numbers
$\overline{R}$	R Bar	The average of the ranges
ROI	ROI	Return on the investment
RQL	RQL	Reject quality level
s	s or 1 sigma	Standard deviation of the population or the width of one zone in the normal distribution curve or 68% of the values. It is calculated as follows:

$$s = \sqrt{\frac{\sum (x-\overline{x})^2}{n-1}}$$

Symbol	Read	Meaning
6 s	6 sigma	A statistical measure expressing how close a product comes to its quality goal of being 99.999997% perfect, that is, 3.4 defects or "off-products" per million parts or units.
s_2	s sub 2	Mean variance
S	S	Standard deviation of the sample
SPC	SPC	Statistical process control

Symbol	Read	Meaning
SQC	SQC	Statistical quality control
TQA	TQA	Total quality assurance
TQC	TQC	Total quality control, that is the application of quality principals to all company endeavors, including satisfying internal customers. Sometimes TQC is referred to as Total Quality Management (TQM).
TQI	TQI	Total quality improvement
TQM	TQM	Total quality management
u	u chart	A type of attribute chart used to track the average number of defects per unit.
USL	USL	Upper specification limit. This statistic is equal to 3 standard deviations above the mean
UCL	UCL	Upper control limit (see below)
UCL/LCL	UCL/LCL	A statistic calculated from the process data to provide a guideline to signal when the population shifts. For the average chart, it is calculated by multiplying the average range by the A sub 2 value and adding or subtracting from the Average of the average range the X double bar value.
USL/LSL	USL/LSL	A statistic, specification limit, to describe the functional requirements set by the customer.
UPL	UPL	Upper process limit. The value is calculated by adding the 3 sigma value to the grand average, that is, X double bar.

Symbol	Read	Meaning
UPL/LPL	UPL/LPL	A statistic, process limit, to describe the inherent variation of the process due only to chance causes. It is equal to $+$ or $-$ the 3 sigma values.
X	X	A number representing the value of a single item
$\overline{X}$	X Bar	Average
$\overline{X}$-R	X bar R	The average $(\overline{X})$ and range (R) chart, a type of variable chart that uses averages and ranges to show whether the process needs to be adjusted or left alone.
$\overline{\overline{X}}$	X double Bar	Average of the averages.
Z	Z	Number of standard deviation units that a particular point is away from the mean. It is calculated as follows: $$Z = \frac{\text{Particular point-mean}}{\text{Standard deviation}}$$
Σ	Sum	Sum of a series of numbers or mearsurements

APPENDIX II

TQM Terms and Terminologies

Acceptable Quality Level — Minimum number of parts or containers that must comply with quality standards, usually stated as percentage.

Acceptance Number — The maximum number of deviations permitted in a sample of a lot that meets a specification.

Assignable cause or special causes — Causes that the operator can do something about. They are detectable and are not always active in the process.

Attribute — An inherent characteristic of a product classfied as acceptable or unacceptable.

Attribute Chart — A type of chart in which characteristics are considered acceptable or acceptable, good or bad, go or no go. The p-chart is an example of an attribute chart.

Attribute Data — Data that comes from nonmeasurable characteristics which can be counted.

Average $(\overline{X})$ — The sum of a number of measurements divided by the number of measured units. It is another term for mean.

Average and Range Chart, $(\overline{X})$ and (R) Chart — The most commonly used variable chart where the average and range are plotted separately over time.

Bimodial distribution — A pattern of variation that appears to have two peaks or humps. This type of distribution is usually the result of a mixture of distributions.

Brainstorming — A group problem solving method to bring out many ideas in a short time.

Capable — If the process spread (6 standard deviations) is less than the customer's specification range, then the process is capable.

c-Chart — A type of attribute control chart that helps monitor the number or count of defects item by item, or by inspection units, in a production run.

Capability Index (C sub p and C sub pk) — The number that expresses the capability of a process or machine. An index used by firms to measure their improvement as they seek greater uniformity around the desired target. It is calculated by dividing the specification width by the process width. The greater the number the better the index.

Capability ratio — The ratio of the machine or process spread (6 sigma) to the specification tolerance, expressed in percent.

CEDAC Cause and Effect Diagram and Cards — A picture diagram to show the many causes that many have an effect on a given problem. Also, known as the "fishbone chart".

Chance Cause or System Cause — Causes that the operator can usually do nothing about because they are built into the process.

Characteristic — Variable attributes that distinguish products.

Chi Square — a statistic used to measure the discrepancy between a set of observed frequencies and their corresponding expected frequencies.

Coefficient of Variability (CV) — a measure of variation of observations that has been adjusted for sample magnitude so that variation between samples with different magnitude can be compared. It may be calculated by dividing the Standard Deviation by the average times 100. Thus, the CV value is expressed in percent.

Competitive benchmarking — Rating a firm's practices, processes, and products against the world's best.

Control Chart — A graphic presentation where one measured characteristic of a process is plotted over time to help detect "process drifts" or deviations. The control chart has a central line representing the average designated by X bar and control limits representing what the process can do when operating consistently. The control limits (upper and lower) are calculated statistically using actual data from the process.

Correlation — The relationship between two factors such as height and weight, color and maturity, etc. The correlation coefficient ("r") is expressed as a decimal value ranging from -1 to +1. If "r" equals zero there is no correlation and values approaching 1 indicate a near perfect relationship. Correlations less than 0.7 are generally not practically significant to draw positive conclusions about the relationships.

Covariance — Varying together

Dependent variable — That variable for which a solution is sought from a knowledge of the value of one or more correlated independent variables.

Deviant — A sample unit affected by one or more deviations or one that varies in a specially defined manner from the requirements of a standard, specification, or other inspection document.

Duplicates — Results from units of experiments made under the same conditions.

Factorial Experiment — An experiment in which the treatments are arranged in all possible combinations.

Fishbone Diagram — Also, known as the Cause and Effect Diagram.

Flow Chart — A step by step depiction of the unit operations in a process.

Frequency Distribution — The pattern formed by a group of measurements of the same kind of units when the measurements are arranged according to how many times each one occurs.

Histogram — A bar diagram representing a frequency distribution of a particular attribute that is measured in the process or of a product.

Independent Variable — A variable which on the basis of a previously established relationship with a dependent variable, may be used for the solution of specific values of the dependent variable.

Inherent Variation — The natural variation in a process due to chance causes.

Interaction — The tendency for the combination of two factors to produce a result that is different from the mere sum of the two individual contributions.

Just in Time — Delivery of materials and supplies as the factory needs them, thus eliminating costly inventories and possible use of last minute defective materials.

Lot — Any number of containers of the same size and type which contain a product of the same type and style located in the same warehouse or conveyance, or which, under in-plant (in-process) inspection, results from consecutive production within a plant, and which is available for inspection at any one time.

Lower Control Limit (LCL) — The lower boundary above which points plotted on a control chart can vary without the need for correction or adjustment.

Mean (Average) (X bar) — Defined as the quotient obtained by dividing the sum of a set of readings or observations by the number of observations.

Mean Square — An estimate of the population variance.

Median — This is the reading or observation above or below which an equal number of observations fall.

Mode — The value that occurs most frequently in a set of data.

np — Average number of defective units for the process. It is obtained by dividing the number of defective units in all samples by the number of samples taken.

np Chart — A chart used to monitor the number of defective units in a production run.

Normal Curve or Distribution — The distribution of individual values with the average, median, and mode the same. Further, the standard deviation divides the range of the set of data into six equal parts. The curve is shaped like a bell and the distribution is sometimes called a bell-shaped curve.

Objective — Capable of being recorded by physical instruments, not dependent upon the observer. Free from personal feelings or prejudice.

Operating Characteristic Curve — The curve that gives the probability of acceptance of a lot on the basis of a specified sampling plan.

p — Average percent defective for the process, that is, the total number of defectives divided by the total number of units inspected and multiplied by 100. The value is expressed as a percentage.

p-Chart — A type of attribute control chart that helps to monitor or control the percent or fraction defective pieces in a production run.

Parameter — A numerical characteristic of a population, estimated by a statistic, such as, average, range, or standard deviation.

Pareto Chart — A bar chart to show the ranking of all potential problems or data or sources of variations where the points are prioritized by the degree of impact on quality and the trivial many are separated from the vital few.

Poka-yoke — Making the workplace mistake proof, that is, fitting the machine or part in such a way that it is can only work one way.

Population — All of the output of a proces over a defined time period.

Precision — Refers to the standard deviation, coefficient of variability, or relative precision. The smaller the value the greater the precision. The closer the agreement between duplicates, the higher the precision.

Probability — The likelihood or chance that something will happen.

Probability Plot — A method for estimating how well the measurements used to make the average and range chart fit a normal curve. This technique, also, estimates the shape of the distribution.

Process — The people, materials, machines (equipment), methods, and environment that produce a product or service.

Process Capability — A statistic used to measure the ability of a process to manufacture a product to a given specification. Usually measured by comparing the spread to 6 sigma values.

Process Spread — The width of the curve formed by the frequency distribution. When compared to the specifications, the process spread tells whether the process can make the product with the specifications. Also, described as the 6 sigma value.

Qualitative Factor — A factor in which the different levels cannot be arranged in order of magnitude, such as, batches, methods, or materials produced in different plants.

Quality — The combination of attributes or characteristics of a product that have significance in determining the degree of acceptability of that product by the user.

Quality Audit — To verify or examine products or processes for compliance to specifications.

Quality Assurance — Processes and products that are acceptable and in conformance to requirements.

Quality Circle — A group of people who meet together on a regular basis to identify, analyze, and solve quality and other problems related to their work.

Quality Control — The regulation of processes and operations to some standard or specification; a tool for the production worker to control the unit operation, line, and or process to some standard or specification.

Quality Evaluation — To describe or appraise the worth of a product according to some standard or specification, generally taking the measurements of a product in the laboratory.

Quantitative Factor — Factors which can be arranged in order of magnitude, such as, temperature, pressure, or items measured on a numerical scale.

Quality function deployment — A system that pays special attention to the wants of the customers.

Random Numbers — Numbers from a table of random numbers used for sampling purposes.

Random Sampling — Samples that are taken in such a way that each member of the lot or population have an equal chance of being selected.

Range (R) — Difference between upper and lower limit of a set of observations. It is one method of measuring the amount of variation.

Rejection Number — The minimum number of deviants in a sample that will cause a lot to fail a specific requirement.

Replication — A part of an experiment containing all the levels of all the factors only once. Sometimes called a block design.

Robust design — A discipline for making process designs "production proof" by building in tolerances for given manufacturing variables that are known to be unavoidable.

Run Chart — A chart used to visually represent data, to monitor a process, to display trends over time.

Sample — A representative set of products ordinarily selected at random from a larger set called a lot and used for inspection or evaluation.

Sampling — The act or practice of selecting samples from a lot for the purpose of inspection.

Sigma ( ) — Symbol for the standard deviation. One sigma means 68% of the products are acceptable, two sigma means that 95% are acceptable, three sigma means that 99% are acceptable while 6 sigma means that 99.999997% are perfect, that is, 3.4% defects units in million.

Skewed Distribution — A pattern of variation that looks almost like a normal distribution except that it is tailed or slanted to one side.

Specification — A specification is basically a communication tool to define reasonable expectations. A specification serves as the body of rules for the manufacture and sale of food products. A specification describes the product, process, or material in specific terms. It should always be written and it should always be objective.

Standard Deviation (Sigma) — A special calculation that describes how closely the measurements cluster around the middles of the normal curve. The number is useful in describing the process spread.

Statistic — An estimate of a parameter, based on a given sample. A sample average is a statistic as is a sample standard deviation or range.

Statistical process control (SPC) — A method of analyzing deviations in production processes during manufacture.

Statistical quality control (SQC) — A method of analyzing measured deviations in manufactured materials, parts, and products.

Subjective — Pertaining to an individual experience which can be observed and reported only by the person involved.

Taguchi methods — a statistical technique for optimizing design and production, often used on "robust design" projects. Named for Genichi Taguchi, a Japanese consultant that developed this technique.

Total Quality Control (TQC) — The application of quality principles to all company endeavors. TQC is primarily the responsibilities of the Quality Assurance personnel. Today, Management requires that employees be trained to operate and control their unit operations and be held accountable for their aspect of the production. Today, QA personnel have the prime responsibilities of training personnel and working on projects to improve the process, thus, the modern concept to describe quality control today is, Total Quality Management (TQM).

Total Quality Management (TQM) — The modern philosophy of management whereby everyone contributes to giving the customer what they expect all the time. It is a system of gauging a firm's dedication to constant improvement to serve the customer with direct emphasis on communication between management, employees, and the customer.

Trivial Many — The majority of causes of variation or cost that only account for a small part of the total variation or cost.

Upper Control Limit — The upper boundary below which points plotted on a control chart can vary without the need for change or correction.

Variable — Procedures based on actual values in terms of numerical scales in contrast to attributes where each item is designated merely as acceptable or unacceptable.

Variable Chart — A type of chart on which measurements are plotted in numbers, that is an average and range chart.

Variance — A measure of variation equal to the square of the standard deviation or its estimate.

Vital Few — The few causes of variation or cost that account for most of the total variation or cost. These are the causes of variation that should be worked on first to solve problems.

REFERENCES

Anon. 1985 Toward Total Quality Control. Quality Control Supervisor's Bull. 822, National Foreman's Institute, Waterford, CT.

Anon. 1990. The Tools of Quality Part IV: Histograms. Quality Progress, September, 75-78.

Anon. 1990. The Tools of Quality Part V: Check Sheets. October, 51-56

Anderson, Larry H. 1990. Controlling Process Variation is Key to Manufacturing Success. Quality Progress, August 91-93.

Bemowski, Karen. 1988. People: The Only Thing that will make Quality Work. Quality Progress. September, 63-67.

Bemowski, Karen. 1990. Closing the Gap. Quality Progress, November 17-20.

Box, George E. P. and S. Bisgaard. 1987 The Scientific Context of Quality Improvement. Quality Progress, June 54-61.

Brick, J. Michael, J. R. Michael, and D. Morganstein. 1989. Using Statistical Thinking to Solve Maintenance Problems. Quality Progress, May 55-60.

Burr, John T. 1990. The Tools of Quality Part I: Going with the Flow (Chart), Quality Progress, June 64-67.

Burr, John T. 1990. The Tools of Quality Part VI: Pareto Charts. Quality Progress, November 59-61.

Carr, Wendell E. 1989. Modified Control Limits. Quality Progress, January 44-48.

Cary, Mark et al 1987. The Customer Window. Quality Progress, June 36-42

Cantello, Frank X, John E. Chambers and James E. Evans. 1990 Evolution to an Effective and Enduring SPC System. Quality Progress, February 60-64

Dew, John R. 1991. In Search of the Root Cause. Quality Progress, March 97-102.

Gibson, Thomas C. 1987. The Total Management Resource. Quality Progress, November 62-66.

Gibson, Thomas C. 1990. Helping Leaders Accept Leadership of Total Quality Management. Quality Progress, November 45-47.

Gibson, Thomas C. 1990. Helping Leaders Accept Leadership of Total Quality Management. Quality Progress, 45-47.

Gitlow, Howard S., S. J. Gitlow, A. Oppenhelm, and R. Oppenhelm. 1990 Telling the Quality Story. Quality Progress, September 41-46.

Gould, Wilbur A. Glossary for the Food Industries. CTI Publications, Inc. Baltimore, MD.

Gould, Wilbur A. 1991. Total Quality Management-A Key to Better Production, Part I. Food Production Management, April, 18-19.

Gould, Wilbur A. 1991 Total Quality Management-A Key to Better Production, Part II. Food Production Management, May, 20-21.

Gould, Wilbur A. 1991. Research and Development Guidelines for the Food Industries. CTI Publications, Inc., Baltimore, MD.

Gould, Wilbur A. and Ronald W. Gould 1988. Total Quality Assurance for the Food Industries. CTI Publications, Inc., Baltimore, MD.

Gunter, Bert. 1989. Statistically Designed Experiments Part I: Quality Improvement, the Strategy of Experimentation, and the Road to Hell. Quality Progress, December 63-64.

Gunter, Bert. 1990. Statistically Designed Experiments Part 2: The Universal Structure Underlying Expermintation. Quality Progress, February, 87-89.

Gunter, Bert. 1990. Statistically Designed Experiments Part 4: Multivariate Optimization. Quality Progress, June 68-69

Gunter, Bert. 1990. Statistically Designed Experiments Part 5: Robust Process and Product Design and Related Matters. Quality Progress. August, 107-108.

Gunter, Bert. 1989. The Use and Abuse of Cpk, Part 3. Quality Progress, May 79-80.

Gunter, Bert. 1991. Process Capability Studies Part 3. The Tale of the Charts. Quality Progress, June 77-85.

Gunter, Berton H. 1989. The Use and Abuse of Cpk. Quality Progress, January 72-73.

Harrignton, Jim 1991 Total Quality: Taking the First Step. Prepared Foods, May 49-51

Harwood, Charles C. and G. R. Pieters. 1990. How to Manage Quality Improvement. Quality Progress, 45-48.

Hopen, Deborah L. 1991. The Process of Communitcating. Quality Progress, June 48-50.

Hunn, Michael S. and Steven I. Meisel. 1991. Internal Communication: Auditing for Quality. Quality Progress, June 56-60.

Jaehn, Alfred H. 1991. The Zone Control Chart. Quality Progress, July 65-68

Juran, J. M. 1991. Strategies for World-Class Quality. Quality Progress, March 81-85.

Karabatsos, Nancy 1989. Quality in Transition, Part One. Quality Progress, December 22-26.

Karabatsos, Nancy 1990. Quality in Transition, Part Two. Quality Progress, January 22-25.

Kenworthy, Harry W. 1986. Total Quality Concept: A Proven Path to Success. Quality Progress, July 21-24.

Krishnamoorthi, K. S. 1989. Predict Quality Cost Changes Using Regression. Quality Progress, December 52-55.

Leppelmeir, John W. 1987. A Common-Sense Approach to SPC. Quality Progress, October 62-64.

Lowe, Frederick E. Lowe 1985. SPC and the Plant Information System. Quality Progress, September, 15-17.

Lubbers, Randall W. and Janice L. Pastoor 1991. Write it Down. Quality Progress, June 34-36.

Luthens, Fred. 1990. Quality is an HR Function. Personnel, May 72.

Mayo, John S. 1986. AT7t: Management Questions for Leadership in Quality. Quality Progress, April 34-39.

McLaurin, Donald L. and Shareen Bell. 1991. Open Communication Lines Before Attempting Total Quality. Quality Progress. June, 25-28.

Moen, Ronald D. and T. W. Nolan. 1987. Process Improvement. Quality Progress, September 62-68.

Mozer, Clark 1984. Total Quality Control: A route to the Deming Prize. Quality Progress, September 30-33.

Nolan, Thomas W. and Lloyd P. Provost 1990. Understanding Variation. Quality Progress, May 70-78

Pavsidis, Constantine 1984. Total Quality Control: An Overview of Current Efforts. Quality Progress, September 28-29.

Persico, John, Jr. 1989. Team up for Quality Improvement. Quality Progress, January 33-37.

Persico, John Jr., Betty L. Bednarczyk and David P. Negus. 1990. Three Routes to the Same Destination: TQM Part 1. Quality Progress, February 29-33.

Persico, John Jr., Betty L. Bednarczyk and David P. Negus. 1990. Three Routes to the Same Desitination: TQM Part 2. Quality Progress, February 37-41.

Priestman, Sarah. 1985. SQC and JIT: Partnership in Quality. Quality Progress, May 31-32.

Propst, A. L. 1987. The Process Qualification Study. Quality Progress, June 70-74.

Quimbny, Charlie, Lynda Parker and A. M. Weimerskirch. 1991. How, Exactly, Do you Communicate Quality. Quality Progress, June 52-54.

Relyea, Douglas B. 1989. The Simple Power of Pareto. Quality Progress, May 38-39.

Robinson, Charles B. 1990. Part 1. Companies Need a Quality Policy. Quality Progress, January 62.

Sarazen, J. Stephen. 1990. The Tools of Quality Part II: Cause and Effect Diagrams. Quality Progress, July 59-62.

Sargent, Terry R. 1986. The Pygmalion Effect on Quality. Quality Progress, August 34-38.

Scholtes, Peter R. and Hero Hacquebord. 1988. Six Strategies for Begining the Quality Transformation, Part II. Quality Progress, August, 44-48.

Shainin, Peter D 1990. The Tools of Quality Part III: Control Chart. Quality Progress, August, 79-82.

Snee, Ronald D. 1986. The Pursuit of Total Quality. Quality Progress, 25-31.

Stein, Bernard. 1991. Management by Quality Objectives. Quality Progress, July 78-80.

Stevick, G. E. 1990. Preventing Process Problems. Quality Progress, 67-73.

Stowell, Daniel M. and H. Scotti Smith. 1991. The Quality Interview. Quality Progress, June 38-41.

Stratten, A. Donald. 1990. Kaizen and Variability. Quality Progress, April 44-45.

Sullivan, L. P. 1984. Reducing Variability: A New Approach to Quality. Quality Progress, July 15.

Tunner, Joseph R. 1987. Total Manufacturing Process Control-The High Road to Product Control. Quality Progress, October 43-50.

Varian, Tom. 1991. Communicating Total Quality Inside the Organization. Quality Progress, June 30-31.

INDEX

INDEX

NOTES

NOTES

NOTES